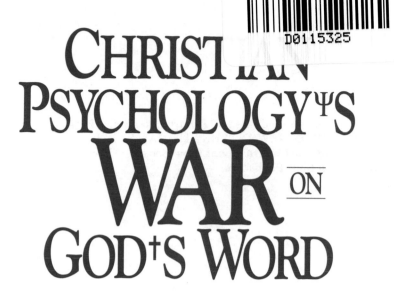

# CHRISTIAN PSYCHOLOGYΨS WAR <u>ON</u> GODᵗS WORD

# THE VICTIMIZATION OF THE BELIEVER

## Jim Owen

EastGate Publishers
Santa Barbara, CA 93110

**CHRISTIAN PSYCHOLOGY'S WAR ON GOD'S WORD
THE VICTIMIZATION OF THE BELIEVER**

Copyright © 1993 James D. Owen
Published by EastGate Publishers
4137 Primavera Road
Santa Barbara, CA 93110

Library of Congress Catalog Card Number 93-070361
ISBN 0-941717-08-9

**Printed in the United States of America**

To my wife of thirty-one years,

Roberta,

who has lived with this book from
its inception until its publication,
and has done so with loving patience
and wifely encouragement.

Proverbs 31:10-12

## Acknowledgements

Many people have contributed to the making of this book—more than I can possibly mention here. But these that are mentioned below have been especially helpful by reading portions, or even the whole manuscript, correcting grammar, offering advice, giving encouragement, time and ears, while I discussed the direction I wanted the book to take. I am indebted and grateful for their involvement.

## Thank you

Bryan Allen, Greg Braley, Martin and Deidre Bobgan, Doug Bookman, Cathy Cornelison, Derek and Michelle Darrow, Joni Frey, John Hotchkiss, Cheryl Markowitz, Cyndi Myles, Linda Paine, Will Patton, Ed Quirley, John Stead, Dave and Kathleen Thomson, Mark and Kayleen Todd.

# CONTENTS

# Prologue

## *Letter to an Imaginary Friend*

This book is bound to stir up controversy—perhaps even heated and passionate controversy. But considering the nature of the subject, such seems inevitable. The presuppositions and counseling methods of psychology have become so integrated into evangelical thinking at every level that to venture criticism is to invite wrath and censure. The "discovered" truths practiced by "Christian" psychology are fast approaching the status once reserved for Scripture.[1] A very dangerous development indeed.

In searching for a way to introduce the "radical" ideas articulated in this book, the concern uppermost in my mind was how to emphasize the destructive results of supposedly integrating the presuppositions of psychology with Scripture. I was opposing strongly held beliefs and practices of fellow believers. How does one overcome that common human reluctance of having one's cherished misconceptions opened to needed correction?

I decided to begin as if I were writing to an old friend who is no longer as close as he once was. He has gone his own way, becoming the consummate Christian psychologist— eclectic and committed to bringing together the humanly "discovered truths" of psychology with the God-revealed truths of Scripture. So dedicated is he to this procedure that he fails to discern the inherent contradiction between the two. Nor does he seem to grasp the unbiblical implications that haunt his counseling techniques.

His desire to help "hurting" people has allowed the end (restoring people) to dictate his means (using a humanistic philosophy to diagnose and cure "sick" people).

While my friend is fictional, his counseling psychology is very real and widely accepted in the evangelical community. If the profile of my "friend" seems to fit any of my readers, I would kindly ask them to give serious thought to the objections I marshal against "Christian" psychology.

## The New Christianity?

"For the times, they are a-changin'." Do you remember those words? If memory serves me, they come from a Bob Dylan song of a generation past. In the turmoil of the late sixties, they were on the lips of dissenters of every hue and stripe who paraded the streets and cursed the establishment. That particular line came to mind last night as I thought about all that I will be writing to you.

To my sorrow, and perhaps yours, I confess my words will not be pleasant. For times are changing in our evangelical community—and you epitomize that change. I find myself concerned with the results. No, *concerned* is too feeble a word. I am much more than concerned. I am perturbed by the transformation taking place. I am perturbed and fearful, alarmed and angry. Perhaps that's too many negatives, but they are justified. Hear me out as I explain why.

I wish I could say that what you are doing is wonderful, but I won't because I can't. Of late, I have been listening to you closely, studying your books, reading and rereading your letters, thinking through again and again your ideas and arguments. I have been listening with increasing tension, noticing how you have eased ever so subtly away from Scripture as the authoritative and sufficient Word from God that could be trusted no matter what the issue or circumstance.

Is the deceitful heart of modern man really too complex to be changed by the simplicity of Scripture alone? I think you have come to believe this is so. "Yes, man is a sinner," I think you would say, "but he is also a victim." In fact, you are more concerned with the latter than the former. Man-the-victim. What a doleful commentary on 20th century man. There are no more heroes, are there? Even more, what a sad commentary on man who is made in the image and likeness of God. Man-the-victim—a concept that conjures up a whole new interpretation of man and his problems. An extrabiblical view of man as it were. One that keeps Scripture at a distance, that even makes it seem prosaic and limited in its application to man's "deepest" needs.

It saddens me to say this, but it seems to me that you have lost that which you once exhibited so boldly: a confidence, a passion in the efficacy of Scripture—yea, in the Lord of Scripture—to change the sinful heart and heal its corruption.

Oh, I hear your protests. You will insist that you believe in the Bible as much as I do. You even quote it to support your arguments. But when you do so I am often left wondering if we are reading the same book. I struggle with the way you handle Scripture and watch with increasing frustration as biblical categories are reconstituted into psychological ones—as if by doing so they have been improved and made more efficacious.[2]

Yes, the times, they are a-changin'.

## What Has Happened?

The nurture of the Scriptures, the wonder and power of prayer, fellowship with other believers in the Spirit, the obedience of self-denial, the longing to see our Lord, to hasten His return, and that joy inexpressible and glorious no matter the circumstances because we are His—all these have been the cherished friends of every true believer across the generations. They have bound us together in a holy comradery that has ignored time and death and culture. Seven ageless friends, we might say, helping us grow in grace, say no to sin by grace, and bear fruit for Jesus' namesake by grace.

What has happened, then, that so many now find them so insignificant, so flawed, so feeble, so powerless to touch the "deep hurts of the heart," as you express it? At what point in our century did grace finally cease to abound much more than sin? When did firm expectations of Jesus' authority to deliver us become nostalgic foolishness?

Or do you think our faith has unfairly demanded more than grace is able or ever intended to give? Or perhaps our sin, our 20th century sin, has indeed become so complex that our faith will not allow us to trust ourselves entirely to the support of such traditional companions? Whatever the case, something more is needed, you insist—and something more is available. "Discovered" truths to compliment and complete the tattered hopes of revealed truth. In this instance, the "discovered" truths of psychology. *Behavioral science* is the term you often use. A term loaded with fascinating implications for the struggling believer. Sin overcome and controlled by science. Who would have ever imagined it? Methodology replacing faith and scientific certainty shoring up the uncertainties of grace.

And those who doubt your new wisdom, who hold to the sufficiency of Scripture, pay a price. They are made to appear stale and uninformed with their dated expectations of God's promises and power. It is amazing how many Christians, when they hear the word *science*, begin to doubt and fret and question the reliability of Scripture. Immediately they set about to find some means to get Scripture to "agree" with science, lest God Himself be seen as outdated and ignorant.

Who dares argue with science, even so dubious a science as psychology? Who wants to be thought a fool? Not many. Though one would think that for Christ's sake someone wouldn't mind being a fool. But perhaps not today. I think the fairy tale about the emperor's new clothes best sums it up. Do you remember it? No one wanted to appear the fool because only fools could fail to appreciate the new and richly embroidered—and non-existent—clothes prepared for the vain ruler. Neither the prime minister, nor the imperial general, nor all the people of the empire, nor even the emperor himself was willing to be convinced by the obvious. Too much was at stake. "Are the others wiser than I," each asked himself in turn. "Is it possible that I am a fool? If so no one must know."[3] And no one did until a young child cried out, "But he's naked," as the emperor marched by in grand procession, as naked as the day he was born.

Such is the power of intimidation and self-serving persuasion. I wonder—are we witnessing a like conformity in the evangelical community? "All truth is God's truth," claims "Christian" psychology, "whether discovered or revealed," as if to make the claim settles the question of its validity and makes holy all it says and does. I can't help being astonished by such confidence. Is it not true there are hundreds of personality theories and virtually thousands of psychological techniques? How do you determine which, if any, are truly God's truth?

## A Hybrid Gospel

The time has come to confront you about these things. A dangerous philosophy is abroad in our community. I fear you and your friends are sowing tares of confusion in believers' minds, moving them to doubt the sufficiency of the words of the One who saved them.

I am convinced you are preaching a hybrid gospel and I am angry about it. You are preaching another gospel, a gospel that leaves us all dependent on you and your methods for the experience of true Christian liberty. Once we were told we could do nothing without Christ. Now we almost hear that Christ can do nothing in us or for us without the help of "Christian" psychology. Even the Holy Spirit is pictured as ineffectual without the right counseling methods. Should I not be perturbed? Should I not be angry?

And I am alarmed because I am not sure you know what you are doing. I cannot believe you are doing this deliberately. You seem so taken with your "discovered truth," so charmed with your "expanded" gospel, so at ease with what you have done, that you can no longer see how far you have stepped off the path.

This alarms me because I believe you love Christ as I do. I believe your motives are sincere—that you care about people and long to help them. And you do so in a limited way . . . or do you? This is the question that will not leave my mind.

I could almost wish you were not the sincere Christian I believe you to be. Then the hard things I must say would not be so hard to say. But as I study your writings, as I listen to your programs, as I observe the impact you have upon the body of Christ, **I am alarmed!**

I will not hide from you what is in my mind and heart. I do not wish to play cat-and-mouse word games with you—trying first one word and then another, all the while hoping to avoid saying straight out, "My friend, the emperor is naked!"

Let me etch in bold relief the issue between us so that you will not be tempted to think I exaggerate or that our differences are little or that these are simply matters of semantics.

The issue is not the validity of counseling as such, nor that many believers are struggling desperately with debilitating sinful attitudes and behavior. Many are—the shocking thing is how many—and we will discuss the reason for this sad state of affairs later. The issue at hand is this: any method of teaching or counseling used supposedly to help a believer overcome sinful behavior, or to progress in his or her sanctification (whether done on an individual basis or in a group), that is not saturated with, limited by, and resting upon the explicit Word of God, has no right to call itself Christian or biblical. Moreover, any method of teaching or counseling that derives its definition of our problems from humanistic presuppositions, which ignore, compromise, alter or downplay the clear teachings of Scripture, and uses methods of treatment based upon such presuppositions must be regarded as nonchristian, extrabiblical, and unscriptural. Yet you, my friend, are committed to, and are practicing, such a system.

## Christ Only

Despite the veneer of a Christian vocabulary, you do not treat reality as essentially spiritual. You do not regard the awesome and mysterious dimensions of the spirit as primary. When all is said and practiced, your world view is basically horizontal. With flesh against flesh, parents against their children, and this generation victimizing the next, the past not only gives birth to a deformed present, but holds it in bondage.

Spiritual reality for you seems to be only so much stage propping; necessary perhaps, but only as a backdrop while center stage you treat the real problems of "personality disorders" with a script borrowed from humanistic psychology.

Whether you intend it or not, your methodology makes Jesus a background savior, whose power is unavailable in our weaknesses, except as mediated through your methods. You become indispensable for the believer's well-being in Christ. The results? Psychology is exalted. Scripture is brought down! I am sorry this sounds so harsh. But it is difficult to sound friendly when I read passages like this one, penned by a colleague of yours:

> Reminders of God's love and exhortations to meditate on Jesus' care sometimes provide about as much help as handing out recipes to people waiting in a food line.[4]

Not exactly a sterling recommendation for our Lord in a moment of crisis, is it? Nor an expression of confidence in His promise.

Certainly there are those who point hurting people to Christ with as much compassion and healing grace as a brick. Yet Scripture does indeed exhort us to remember God's love and Christ's perseverance when our circumstances seem overwhelmingly painful. (See 2 Thessalonians 3:5.)

"Trust in him at all times, O people," wrote the psalmist. "Pour out your hearts to him, for God is our refuge" (Psalm 62:8). If this is what God desires us to do, why should such an exhortation offend us or fail to lift us up? Why should we consider it less than adequate for our immediate needs? Why, instead, should we seek relief in self-pity or self-indulgence or some other human solution?

You are my friend and brother in Christ. Yet true friendship demands I first be loyal to my Lord Jesus and His Word and call you to do the same. You stand on dangerous ground. Something John Bunyan wrote best sums up my position. "Christ and Christ only," he wrote, "can make us capable of enjoying God, with life and joy for all eternity."[5] What a profound and eloquent testimony to the sufficiency of the Lord of Glory. Lord of Glory—what a title! What promises that title contains!

I have come to relish Bunyan's words because I have come to love the Scriptures. And I love them because I love the Lord of the Scriptures. This is all His doing. He alone is to rule my life through His Word, ministered to me by His Spirit. "My grace is sufficient for you," He said to me, "for my power is made perfect in weakness" (2 Corinthians 12:9). I believe this. I have experienced this.

Yet I make no claim to spiritual superiority. I neither believe in nor love my Lord with all the passion He deserves. To my deep shame, I admit that too often I have been turned aside by some petty sin. I believe it was John Wesley who said that the Christian's life is all mystery and grace. Jesus is faithful—and that is what matters in the end. Despite my failings, both great and small, His love continues to nurture mine. This is the wonder of His grace. "Christ in you, the hope of glory," Paul wrote (Colossians 1:27). For this reason, we can experience "inexpressible and glorious joy."

How then can I question His words given to me to order every aspect of my life? How can I limit the range of their authority when it is His authority? How can I deny the sufficiency of my King who has promised me He would complete the good work He has begun in me (Philippians 1:6)? So if there is dominating, cherished sin in my life, dare I say, for any reason, that it is too powerful and my Lord too weak? No—let me confess, if I would be true to Scripture, that it is because I love Him too little and my sin too much (though I have a thousand lying disguises to hide my idolatry).

Nor is it, as I have heard some claim, that I would wade heart-deep in wickedness because I think too poorly of myself. Rather it is the reverse—I would secretly exalt myself. (It was not from want of self-esteem that Satan assaulted the throne of God.) Surely I dare not say it is because I have stored, in some cunningly hidden archive of my mind, hurts and disappointments that compel me to satisfy my deepest longings in perverse and rebellious ways. Would not this be the most obvious self-deception of all? Rather let me again confess, again to be true to Scripture, that I sin but for one clear and shameful reason. I deny my King His rightful sovereignty and despise His glory.

There is an ever widening gulf beginning to separate us, my friend. What a quandary you have placed yourself in! On one hand you do not believe in the sufficiency of Scripture alone, yet you dare not let it go altogether. On the other hand, though, you reject humanism as an explanation of reality, you accept its wisdom in the very area you ought to spurn it. The tragedy is that you do not grasp the magnitude of the compromise you have made.

A great folly seems to have overtaken many 20th century evangelicals: they constantly yield the authority and sufficiency of God's Word to the idols of modernity. They concede this portion to an aged evolutionary "science," frayed and dated in its Victorian dress. They concede that portion to the social expediency of the times, fearful lest God's sovereignty in all things might offend the liberal sensibilities of the NOW generation. Will they also concede the wisdom and power of the cross to the heirs of Sigmund Freud? God forbid! Yet it seems many are doing so.

In light of this, how much longer will the church believe in and support the idea of an authoritative Bible to which the followers of Jesus can commit themselves? Five years? Ten? Is it already too late?

Within twenty-five years of the acceptance of Darwinism by the American intellectual community, practically every major seminary capitulated to liberalism. An inerrant revelation from God? Impossible! The virgin birth? Please. The deity of Christ? An attempt by the early church to compete with paganism. The atonement? How bloody and primitive! How can we believe in a God so barbaric?

What was needed, these men in lock-step with the "discovered truths" of their day informed us, was a Christianity more in keeping with the assured results of current "scholarship." Fearing embarrassment, a considerable segment of the American church created just such a Christianity. Forty years later, H. Richard Niebuhr was to write that liberal Christianity was reduced to "a God without wrath (bringing) men without sin into a kingdom without judgment through the ministrations of a Christ without a cross."[6]

These men all believed that "all truth is God's truth." Today, with the rise of "Christian" psychology, likewise mixed with humanism and appealing to the same axiom, I foresee a like collapse within the evangelical community. At present, I doubt that you will agree. However, read this book and I will show you just how far down that path "Christian" psychology has already taken us.

---

## Notes

1     The term *Christian psychology* is a misnomer. There are Christians who are trained psychologists but there is no discipline as such that can be designated Christian psychology, contrasted with, say, secular psychology.

However, the term *Christian psychology* is popular among evangelicals and carries with it the connotation that such a body of knowledge does exist. Thus I put the term *Christian* within quotation marks to draw attention to the fact that it is a mistake to speak of "Christian psychology" as if it were substantively different than humanistic psychology.

2     Let me list a few of these substitute words. *Disease* is one of the most common. It replaces the ideas of a sin nature and being in bondage to lust. *Addiction* is another replacement word. People don't lust anymore, or give themselves over to lusting continually as described in Ephesians 4:19. No—now they are addicted (implying thereby haplessness as well as helplessness). And when they lie about their addiction, they are not really lying. They are just in the denial stage of their disease. One writer wanted to replace the word *idolatry* with the term *addiction*. He believed they expressed the same thing. Another psychologist constantly refers to man's sin nature as his "self-biased impulse drive." *Dysfunctional* is another word substitute for *sin*. People come from "dysfunctional" homes these days and thus have acquired "dysfunctional" behavior.

The term *self-actualization* has been equated with the word *sanctification* and Christ is described as the most self-actualized person in history. The word *reprogramming* is commonly used to explain what the Bible means by the phrase "renewing of your mind" (Romans 12:2). People who use other people and try to control them are no longer guilty of self-glorification. Rather they are sick with "codependency."

On and on we could go. Where we will stop only God knows. Sometimes I think we are caught up in the throes of a great silliness. But it is obvious that biblical terminology is not something we want to use in describing ourselves and our reality. We are becoming less and less "user-friendly" with a vocabulary that holds us 100%

culpable. Mary Ann Bell, in a commentary in *World* magazine, asked this question after a Bible teacher stated
that he wanted to "jump off the biblical diving board into
the 'real stuff of life':

> Are we to believe the precise communication of
> inspired writers is less useful for edification than
> the reality of 20th century language and stuff?
> (Mary Ann Bell, *World*, March 24, 1990, p. 19.)

If the truth were out, that is exactly the way those
Christians think who are immersed in psychology. Biblical language doesn't easily lend itself to a pathologically
defined society. It doesn't give us license to feel and talk
about the hurts and disappointments our defenseless psyches have had to suffer. Words like *disease* and *dysfunctional* and *victim* are much more welcome. Bell concludes
her commentary with these words of warning:

> [A] culture that creates new names for old objects—
> sickness for sin, denial for lying, etc.—conceives for
> itself new ethical realities. The question is: Are we
> ready to live with the results? (p. 19.)

We might also ask ourselves this. Will these ethical realities be biblical?

3   Jean Van Leeuwen, *The Emperor's New Clothes* (New
    York: Random House, 1971).

4   Larry Crabb, *Inside Out* (Colorado Springs: NavPress,
    1988), p. 194.

5   John Bunyan, compiled by Roger C. Palms, *Upon a Penny
    Loaf* (Minneapolis: Bethany Fellowship, Inc., 1978), p. 16.

6   Sydney E. Alhstrom, *A Religious History of the American
    People* (New Haven: Yale University Press, 1972), p. 784.

# 1

# The Sufficient Christ?

"We have met the enemy and he is us." Immortal words uttered by the comic-strip character, Pogo Possum. They are words that might cause a wry smile of acknowledgment to appear briefly on our faces. Too often, much too often, we are our own worst enemy, aren't we? Not our environment, or our past or others or what-have-you. In fact, at times, one can only marvel at the consistency with which human beings "pridefully" practice self-destruction, both collectively and individually. What we build with great effort, we almost casually destroy with a single action—marriages, careers, virtues. The list is depressing. We deliberately smash our thumbs, as it were, with the hammer of our wrong-headedness.

Even with the best of intentions, we seem to be able to create havoc. "The road to hell," the old aphorism goes, "is paved with good intentions." So it is. So also are many of the miseries that attend our daily lives. Perhaps in this up-beat age of positive thinking and self-esteem, we squirm and fret at such a "gloomy" assessment of ourselves. However, would any of us deny that we have a more than nodding acquaintance with Pogo's wisdom?

Even for the believer this is true. While it is certain that we wrestle not (just) against flesh and blood and that there are powerful and malevolent beings arrayed against us, we cannot lay the blame for our failings at their doorsteps. No—reality and Scripture buttress this inescapable truth—"we have met the enemy and he is us." Ministries are destroyed, families shattered, godly individuals scarred, shameful memories haunt us, the Lord's name is maligned and the cross scorned, all because believers choose to be their own worst enemy through pride, selfishness, and even, now and then, good but misguided intentions that should have never been acted upon in a fallen world.

John Bunyan understood Pogo's wisdom long before Pogo uttered it when he wrote:

> I found that I loved Christ dearly. Oh, but my soul cleaved to him, my affections cleaved to him. I felt my love to him as hot as fire. But I quickly found that my great love was but little, and that I who had, as I thought, such burning love for Jesus Christ could let him go again for a trifle.[1]

## A Dangerous Integration

Of late, Pogo's words have settled deeply into my mind with sobering heaviness. It has become my conviction, reinforced by the writing of this book, that the evangelical community is in serious trouble. Oh, outwardly the facade holds firm—we seem to be a biblically driven and Bible believing people. Yet behind the facade an unraveling is taking place. A certain "jadedness" with Scripture is making its authority uncertain. Our faith is slowly becoming nothing more than mere routine as the power and person of Christ slip away into pure abstraction.

Two accelerating trends within the evangelical community bear witness to this conclusion. First is the church's fascination (I could almost say captivity) with American secular culture. Whether it concerns habits of speech or dress or music, ambitions or wants or needs, goals or values or morals, too often there is little to distinguish believer from unbeliever. The centrality of Christ and His cross is being replaced by a preoccupation with ourselves—our happiness, our problems, our rights and our worth. Both the uniqueness of the Gospel and its integrity are being compromised. The price we are paying is high. J. I. Packer once calculated the cost with these words: "Though we negate secular humanist doctrine, we live by its value system and suffer its symptoms."[2] Packer made that comment several years ago, but one would be hard pressed to say the situation has improved. We seem to be a people who do not remember how to separate from error—or do not want to.

Such a state of compromise has led many Christians into lives filled with desperation and shame, self-abuse and endless guilt, sinful habits and bondage to lust. For many professing Christians there is no new creation, no victory, no joy, no praise. Why not? Because there is no reality of the living Christ, whose grace is more than sufficient.

As bad as this is, it is not the worst development. Not only have we embraced humanism's values and suffered its symptoms, but we have gone a step further. We have accepted humanism's diagnosis of what ails the human soul and have eagerly begun to practice the "cure" it prescribes. Nowhere is this more evident than in the presuppositions and counseling methodology of "Christian" psychology.

Over the last decade, the evangelical community's embrace of psychology has been nothing short of mind boggling. It is a discipline that has mesmerized the church. Among the most popular books, tapes, radio and TV programs are those of the Christian psychologists. Their clinics and offices are crowded with troubled and defeated believers. Their seminars are well attended and their videos are viewed with ready acceptance in countless churches across America.

Why do so many embrace "Christian" psychology? Perhaps some are grateful to avoid the obedience of faith. Others follow out of ignorance or intimidation. Some embrace psychology because they are now too well informed to "simply trust in Jesus." Others follow because faith in the reality of the power of Christ eludes them, and they are so desperate to break their bondage to sin that they will gladly try whatever system promises to bring them peace.

If I were asked to name the most influential people within the evangelical church today, I would unhesitantly answer, "Christian psychologists." I would hasten to add, "This is an unparalleled disaster for the church and the Scripture upon which its authority rests."

That is a strong, even judgmental statement. But I do not choose my words casually. The purpose of this book is to show why and how it is an accurate one.

Although "Christian" psychology claims to integrate Scriptural truth with "discovered" (i.e., scientific) truth, integration is not occurring. Integration is virtually impossible. "Christian" psychology sets aside the historical-grammatical method of interpreting Scripture and replaces it with a hermeneutic centered on pathology.

Such a hermeneutic views man not as a sinner but rather as a victim whose victimization has left him with deeply buried feelings of anger and inferiority, which in turn cripple his life through "dysfunctional" behavior. **This approach sees man's fundamental *problem* as ignorance of himself and his psychic injuries, rather than deliberate disobedience to and ignorance of the living and true God**. Man's primary *need* becomes esteeming himself more highly, rather than dying to self and living for God through faith in Christ (Romans 6:8-14).

It is upon these two premises, adopted from humanistic psychology, that "Christian" psychology has built its counseling methodology. **It emphasizes man-as-victim rather than man-as-sinner. Such a view radically challenges the biblical doctrines of man's absolute culpability before the cross, the supremacy of the Holy Spirit in the believer's sanctification, and most importantly the sufficiency and authority of Scripture for the believer**. By advocating a pathological interpretation of man, "Christian" psychology profoundly reinterprets the Gospel—with staggering implications for Christianity.

What is just as astounding, however, is that the evangelical church has so readily and uncritically accepted "Christian" psychology with scarcely a murmur of protest. Adding to my wonder is that "Christian" psychology does not hesitate, both directly and indirectly, to charge the church with **massive insensitivity and failure in truly meeting the "real needs" of its people**. Nor has it been any less critical in its attacks against those who would use Scripture alone to counsel someone enslaved to sin.[3]

## An Impossible Peace

Not long ago I was told, "Scripture just isn't sufficient in every area where people have problems. Scripture doesn't tell me how to counsel the anorexic, for example." The speaker seemed so pleased with himself when he said that, as if an argument had been won before it had begun.

"You're right. That is true," I thought to myself. But Scripture doesn't tell me how to counsel a murderer either, or a swindler, or a fornicator, or any other sinner, except to begin with their self-idolatry, except to place them before the cross and call them to repentance. Not very sophisticated, I know, or scientific or complex. Sadly, I said nothing. I let myself be intimidated even though I was convinced the speaker was wrong.

How I wish that man had been with me a few days later! He would have heard the testimony of a young woman who had been "bulimic." He would have learned how, before Christ found her, she had sought psychological counseling and joined a support group—all to no avail. Then she became a Christian, but still she continued in her sin. So it was back to the psychologist and the support group, only this time they were Christian. Again, it did not work. At last she confessed her hidden behavior to her fiancé. Surprisingly, he took her to the Word of God, confronted her with its commands and promises, and held her accountable to them. At that point, she happily stated, she abandoned her "bulimia" and never turned back to it.

Ah, for those who "simply" believe, the love of God can do astounding and wonderful things. Even today! Yes, He does "break the power of canceled sin." He does "set the prisoner free."

Why is it, though, I sense so many would not be pleased with that young woman's testimony? Why do I imagine them saying she only put a band-aid over her problem, that she only denied the anger and buried the hurts she surely feels?

Why is it that the wonderful and unquantifiable intercession of the Holy Spirit, who applies God's grace and power to the immediate needs and conflicts of the believer and ensures him of victory, seems so foreign to the presuppositions of "Christian" psychology and so absent from its counseling? Is it because He cannot be reduced to a method (an overriding compulsion in psychology) and therefore He can only be ignored or downgraded?

"We have met the enemy and he is us." It has become my firm conviction that "Christian" psychology represents one of the most dangerous challenges to the sufficiency and authority of Christ and His Word that the church has faced this century. A hundred years ago Charles Spurgeon wrote that "inspiration and speculation cannot long abide in peace."[4] The same holds true today regarding the speculation of psychology.

Scripture cannot be endlessly pulled and kneaded and punched, like so much dough, into this shape or that, to fit whatever propositional mold psychology has in mind. Antitheses cannot be ignored all the days of our lives. To do so is to destroy the very heart of biblical Christianity, to empty the cross of Christ of its power.

Scripture simply cannot "abide in peace" with the philosophy that energizes psychology. One cannot make Christian that which is essentially anti-Christian, no matter how Christian its practitioners may be. The presuppositions of psychology, as well as the counseling methodology derived from them, ultimately call into question the life-transforming power of the cross, the life-giving authority of the Scriptures, and the reality of the believer's fullness in Christ. In short, they empty Christ of His glory.

The church so far has been reluctant to face this situation because psychology has so deeply permeated evangelical thought. Can we afford this reluctance much longer? I do not think so. If the church will not take a hard look at "Christian" psychology, then it is well on its way to becoming enmeshed in a modern day heresy.

Basic Christian truths are involved that cannot be bypassed or altered for the sake of unity or for a well-intentioned desire to "heal" those who are hurting. The most basic of these truths is the sufficiency of Christ Jesus. The fundamental reality of the grace of our Lord to break the power of sin is being dangerously questioned under the influence of "Christian" psychology. How long can we deny that something of crucial importance is going on here?

## The Book's Purpose

Most of those who use psychology in their counseling do so with the best of intentions and motives. We live in a culture that is committing moral suicide, in a society where thousands upon thousands of desperate and apparently hapless individuals seem unable to resist evil and destructive lusts. Tragically, this seems almost as true for the evangelical community as for society at large. In such a context, the desire to reach out in Christian compassion is noble and commendable.

"Christian" psychology's intentions may be commendable, but its methodology and the presuppositions upon which it depends are not. The sincerity of an individual's faith or the praiseworthiness of his compassionate intentions does not give him permission to undermine the reality of Jesus Christ and His authority and sufficiency as revealed in His Word and ministered to us by the Holy Spirit. The evangelical community faces a far more serious problem than insensitivity to supposedly victim-driven behavioral problems.

Let me also stress that this book is not about personalities or any individual Christian's character or faith. It is not my intent to "get" anyone. This book is about philosophy and method. I am taking to task specific ideas and practices and how they impact Scriptural truths . . . how they affect you and me. When I quote someone or critique what he has written, do not take it as a personal attack. It is impossible to properly evaluate a subject without offering examples or illustrations. The examples I have chosen are meant only to represent a presupposition and/or method widely accepted and practiced by "Christian" psychology.

Nevertheless, this book is anything but dispassionate. The more I delve into this matter, the deeper becomes my conviction that our Lord is being robbed of His glory, that "Christian" psychology is undercutting His authority and sufficiency, and that it poses a distinct threat to biblical Christianity. How could I be dispassionate under such a conviction?

At heart the book is meant to lift up anew the glorious sufficiency of our Lord Jesus Christ and His Word. The two are inseparable. A Christianity that does not rest upon this foundation alone is not true Christianity.

It is also my prayer that this book might reignite in the heart of many a vibrant and victorious faith in the promises of God found in His Word. When God promises that, when I am tempted, I am also given a way of escape (1 Corinthians 10:13), when Christ tells me that His power is sufficient for me to endure any trial and emerge victorious (2 Corinthians 12:7-10), am I not to believe these words with complete confidence? Or am I to believe those who tell me that these promises cannot always be trusted, that they cannot be effective without the assistance of "Christian" psychology?

By their embrace of and dependence on the methodology of psychology, many Christians are surely close—perhaps ignorantly so—to denying God's great and precious promises. No matter how well-intentioned or helpful the process of psychology appears to be, we deny Christ His rightful glory (and ourselves the experience of His reality) when we place the promises of God in bondage to human interpretations. To our great harm, this is what many are doing.

The truth is, God's word still means what it has always meant. As the author of Hebrews wrote:

> Because God wanted to make the unchanging nature of his purpose very clear to the heirs of what was promised, he confirmed it with an oath. God did this so that, by two unchangeable things in which it is impossible for God to lie, we who have fled to take hold of the hope offered to us may be greatly encouraged. We have this hope as an anchor for the soul, firm and secure. It enters the inner sanctuary behind the curtain, where Jesus, who went before us, has entered on our behalf. He has become a priest forever, in the order of Melchizedek (Hebrews 6:17-20).

And not just any priest, but **my** priest on **my** behalf before **my** Father. Yes, I will boast of this. It is impossible for God to lie. I can trust His promises, without doubt or addition. There is no "but you need more." Jesus is able to deliver from the bondage of sin any who ask—and He will do it. He is doing it!

That any believer would cast doubt on this scriptural truth is deeply, deeply troubling. Even when the intent is to "help," he unintentionally obscures the glorious grace of Christ. Such a state of affairs cannot be ignored or be allowed to flourish as if all is well in the body of Christ.

## Notes

1   John Bunyan, compiled by Roger C. Palms, *Upon a Penny Loaf* (Minneapolis: Bethany Fellowship, Inc., 1978), p. 133.

2   J. I. Packer, "Decadence a la Mode," *Christianity Today* (October 2, 1987), p. 13.

3       If anyone doubts this assertion, I invite him to consider the following. The counseling pastor of a large midwestern church became heavily influenced by, and trained in, the teachings and methods of a particular "Christian" psychologist—so much so that he no longer believed it possible to counsel someone from the Word of God alone.

The senior pastor became concerned and investigated the writings of this psychologist. He came to the strong conclusion that this person's position was not scriptural, and in fact undermined belief in the sufficiency of Scripture to deal with sin. The senior pastor raised this issue with the counseling pastor. What were the results? Let me give them to you in the senior pastor's own words:

> I raised the issue with our staff (10 pastors), our board, and ultimately the whole church. The results were disastrous. The man in charge of our counseling program told me that there was no one on the board or the staff equipped to help people with sin except the people who had been trained in [this psychologist's] approach. Being a mature, godly man with a thorough knowledge of Scripture was not enough!
>
> One of the Board members who had worked closely with our counseling pastor sat down with me and told me that my problem was not with (this psychol-

ogist) and his theology, but that I had sin buried deep down inside and had developed protective layers for self defense. He said I didn't even know it, but if I would allow him, he could help me peel back the layers and deal with it. He made a similar accusation at a board meeting, and the Board said it would be necessary for him to retract the unfounded accusation and apologize or resign. He chose to resign.

The impact upon the church of (this psychologist's) teaching was thorough and devastating. The issue turned from the serious theological issues to personalities. Anyone who opposed (this psychologist) and his approach was said to be unloving and uncaring. If you stood for the sufficiency of the Scripture to deal with sin, you were said to be shallow and insensitive to people.

The above is not an isolated incident. It is happening everywhere in the evangelical community. There is increasing evidence that multiple thousands of Christians are putting their faith in what psychologists tell them rather than in the Word of God.

4 Iain Murray, *The Forgotten Spurgeon* (London: The Banner of Truth Trust, 1973), p. 143.

# 2

# Speaking of Sin

Many believers experience a moment, I think, when the Holy Spirit brings them face to face with the biblical truth that "all have sinned and come short of the glory of God" (Romans 3:23). Overwhelmed by their vileness before the fearful and unfathomable holiness of God, so stunned by it, they sink to their knees in unutterable shame and repentance. But it does not end there. For there follows an overwhelming realization of the depth and breadth and height of God's undeserved mercy and grace given to us in Christ Jesus. So overpowering is this realization that they stay on their knees, adoring, praising and thanking God in all humility and unfeigned gratitude. For one brief moment, this side of eternity, they clearly and deeply grasp the God they worship.

I had such an experience many years ago. It was unique and penetrating and unlike any experience I had ever had. It came upon me so quickly that I found no time to rationalize my response. I was reading the 78th Psalm, when without warning the Holy Spirit revealed to me how much I had mirrored Israel by sinning against the goodness and patience of my God, by arrogantly presuming again and again upon His

Fatherly mercies. Swiftly came the conviction of my betrayal, followed by the wonder of His matchless forgiveness and grace. A verse in one of Philip Bliss's hymns expresses it perfectly:

> Guilty, vile and helpless we,
> Spotless Lamb of God was He,
> Full atonement, can it be?
> Hallelujah, what a Savior![1]

I share this personal, and for me, vital incident for a reason. I want us to concentrate on only one theme—that of sin and sinners. It will not be easy or pleasant. Even as believers, knowing fully the extent of our forgiveness in Christ, it can be difficult to hear Scripture out on this subject. Yet today, as never before, we need to listen to what Scripture has to say. It is in how we are to understand and deal with sin that I find "Christian" psychology's foremost challenge to the authority and sufficiency of the Word of God.

As "Christian" psychology's influence has spread within the evangelical community, so has its influence over how we view sin. It modifies the biblical concept of man-the-sinner with a psychological one of man-the-victim. Further, it modifies the Bible's insistence that man is culpable for his sin with the assertion that man is often helpless to stop his sinful activity without the intervention of psychology.

I often find myself wondering if a modern evangelical congregation could survive Jonathan Edward's sermon, "Sinners in the Hands of an Angry God." There are not too many ego strokes in reminding people of the exceeding sinfulness of sin and the awful state of the sinner in the hands of a holy, wrathful God who hates wickedness and the wicked (Psalm 11:5,6).

Somehow we need to be sobered in our attitude regarding sin. Edward's sermon might do that for us. Even more effective, though, would be Joseph Alleine's classic work, *An Alarm to Unconverted Sinners*. What an uncomfortable book it can be to read! More than once, when I first read it, I had to put it aside for a day or two before continuing. Alleine does not hesitate to draw from the pages of Scripture the awful effect sin has upon mankind and the terrible and wretched condition of a sinner outside of Christ. So wicked and rebellious is that sinner that Alleine imagines creation itself would turn upon him if God would allow it. "If inanimate creatures could but speak," Alleine wrote to the unsaved:

> . . . thy food would say, Lord, must I nourish such a wretch as this, and yield forth my strength for him to dishonor thee? The very air would say, Lord, must I give this man breath to speak against heaven and scorn thy people, and vent his pride and wrath, and filthy communications, and utter oaths and blasphemy against thee? His poor beast would say, Lord, must I carry him upon his wicked design? A wicked man! The earth groans under him, and hell groans for him, till death satisfies both. While the Lord of Hosts is against thee, be sure the host of the Lord is against thee, and all the creatures, as it were, up in arms.[2]

Regretfully, few write with such convicting power today. Sophistication has overtaken us. The stress today is that people are hurting and disappointed and need to hear that God loves them and identifies with their pain. As one Christian psychologist put it, "Yes, Jesus came to save sinners, but He also came to experience what it felt like to be betrayed so He could understand our feelings of being betrayed."[3]

Comments such as this convince me we have become too casual about sin, especially as God sees it. We have made repentance a trivial thing. Consider, for example, the evangelical college students who recently participated in a Gallup poll. They were asked if they disapproved of premarital sex. Forty-eight percent answered, "No."[4] I don't think it would hurt these students to read *Alarm*. Mind you, these were professing Christians. Why do you think they hold such beliefs? Why do they seem to have such a casual opinion of their sin and their God? There are those who would rationalize their behavior on the basis of low self-esteem or of unconscious responses to hidden victimizations. Am I exaggerating? Let me give a few examples and perhaps change your mind.

Before he was married, a youth pastor friend had a divorced roommate. The roommate was getting his life back together in the Lord when he dated a young lady with a background similar to his. At the conclusion of their date, to his surprise she invited him to spend the night with her. When he asked how a Christian woman could make such an offer, she replied that "God had given her a sexual appetite" and it **needed** to be met. To his credit he did not take her up on her offer or take her out again. But I definitely think she needs to read *Alarm* because I am alarmed for her.

One "Christian" radio psychologist told a similarly promiscuous young lady she needed victimization counseling. Though the young lady claimed to be a Christian, she admitted she went to bed with nearly every guy she dated. Immediately the psychologist began asking about her relationship with her parents. How did she relate to her mom? How did she relate to her dad? She replied that she had a love-hate relationship with her mom, who tried to dominate her, while her father was distant and uninvolved with her in any meaningful way.

"See," said the psychologist, with an instant analysis, "your problem is that you are trying to get even with your parents. You are telling them that this is the kind of daughter they have because of the way they raised you." Then he told her she needed counseling.

"Oh," she replied, "I've been in counseling for about a year."

"You will need a lot more than that," answered the psychologist. "You will need two or three years of counseling." He then encouraged the young lady to find a church that would accept and support her during this difficult time.

During the whole conversation there was no call for her to repent of sin, or even a warning that her behavior might evidence a lack of salvation (1 Corinthians 6:9,10). No doubt he would say her behavior was wrong, but he treated her as a victim responding to her victimization. I do believe both the psychologist and the young woman would profit from reading *Alarm*. I find myself echoing the question asked of me by a woman whose husband went through victimization counseling for committing adultery. She participated in the counseling with him only to come away sadly disillusioned. "It is such a pertinent question today," she wrote, "whatever happened to the concept of sin?"

I could stack story upon story to prove my point. Sexual immorality seems especially rampant among evangelicals, and victimization and low self-esteem are commonly identified as the cause. In fact, one noted youth evangelist listed this as the chief reason for teen-age sexual misconduct. Perhaps. But some of the young ladies in a Bible study I once taught would have gladly shared *Alarm* with some "Christian" guys they had dated. The guys encouraged them to "give in" because God had already forgiven them. (Like hey—why deny yourself some fun when your self-esteem is so low and God's grace is so abundant?) One young man reminded his girlfriend that we all sin every day so it is really only a matter of choice.

Do you suppose there is something radically wrong with our view of God's love, our responsibility for our sinfulness, and our understanding of the message of the cross? I do. Do you suppose our constant emphasis on victimization, our low self-esteem and our "needs" might have something to do with it? I do.

If you have doubts, consider the case published in an Ann Landers' column. A young lady, who signed her letter "a crushed Christian in California," started attending a weekly singles' Bible study. There she took up with a young man who was part of the church leadership. She was flattered by his attention and as their relationship deepened, she confided to him that she was about to receive a large sum of money. Shortly thereafter, the young man "revealed" to her that God wanted him to marry her.

After several weeks of "heavy courting," they set a wedding date. From that point on, her fiancé began running her life by saying he knew God's will for her. "I was afraid to contradict him," she writes. Curiously, however, God's will included having him move in with her, giving him money she would normally give to the church, supporting him, buying him clothes, and finally buying him a Jaguar.

What finally broke his spell over her was not any conviction from the Word of God, but rather his "revelation" that God didn't want her to become a nurse, a career she sincerely wanted to pursue. "I finally realized," she admits, "that God did not want me to support a lazy, self-indulgent free-loader, whether he was in the ministry or not." Using God to manipulate her was "cruel and sadistic," she writes.

> My emotional scars will take years to heal and I may never fully trust a minister or church again. My money is gone. I am now undergoing treatment for depression as a result of this nightmare. I suffer from insomnia and suicidal tendencies.[5]

This young woman was selfishly used. But please notice—**not once does she hold herself responsible!** She identifies herself as a Christian, yet never admits to any sin. She never warns other believers that disobeying God's law brings bitter consequences as she herself can testify. She never mentions her own need for repentance. She is only a victim, not a sinner—abused, used and filled with self-pity.

## The New Gospel

"Here is a trustworthy saying that deserves full acceptance," wrote the Apostle Paul. "Christ Jesus came into the world to save sinners—of whom I am the worst" (1 Timothy 1:15). Here is the whole message of the cross in one verse. The four Gospels and twenty-three epistles are masterfully encapsulated in those twenty-four words.

Unfortunately, this message didn't get through to one prospective Christian college student who wrote on the admissions application this answer to why people need Christ: "People need Christ so that they can have a sense of self-esteem and self-worth." Is it possible that this young person came to such a conclusion from the study of Scripture? Who taught this prospective student such a peculiar doctrine about our Lord's death and resurrection?

Perhaps this applicant was influenced by someone similar to a young psychologist I know who recently graduated from a Christian college. This psychologist now works for a mission agency as a counselor. In a prayer letter, this psychologist speaks of the urgent needs of people. An urgent need to hear the Gospel? No, rather for someone to listen to them, someone with whom to share the pain and frustration that fill their lives.

What is missing in this letter (and every letter I have received from this person to date) is any acknowledgment of the reason people are filled with pain and frustration: they are sinners. Not one letter has mentioned that unless these people hear the Gospel and repent, they are going to hell. Not one letter has asked me to pray for their salvation. I believe this young person is born again. I am disturbed by the almost deliberate avoidance of the word "sin" and "sinners."

Perhaps I am being too hard on this fledgling psychologist. Perhaps this beginner has been influenced by someone similar to the clinical psychologist who preached at my church. As he talked, he stood clear of the pulpit so as to "remove any artificial barriers between us." He was warm and personable and sympathetic. He emphasized the pain, hurts, loneliness and disappointments people carry around inside themselves. He spoke of how believers can and must reach out to hurting people with God's love.

In a very real sense, it was a compassionate message. Yet for all his compassion, he never once mentioned that people are lost sinners, lovers of darkness, whose sin has separated them from God's love and caused their hurts. Not once did he mention the word *sin*. Not once did he mention that the most

compassionate words sinners need to hear is that Jesus
Christ died on the cross for their sins. Not once did he mention their eternal destiny if they do not believe the Gospel. I
had the concrete impression that he deliberately left those
words out of his sermon.

Something is getting out of kilter here. A pattern is
emerging in evangelical circles. As more and more people
speak of victims who hurt, we seem to be less and less willing
to speak of them as sinners who sin. This is especially true
where "Christian" psychology is the most influential. Take
the following as one small example.

An advertisement, placed in a leading Christian magazine by a leading Christian publisher, promoted a how-to
book that promised to help us become the best friend anyone
could ever ask for. "The 'you' others welcome," said the ad
copy. It was a "book about skills, hope and lasting change in
your life." (Quite a promise.) Included in the ad was a statement about the basic nature of man. It jarred me deeply
because it was so at odds with Scripture. "Let's be clear," the
ad says:

> *Friendship* is not about guilt. You were created a
> warm, caring, outgoing person. Everyone is. But
> somewhere along the way, you (like the rest of us)
> picked up something else: how not to relate. But
> there's good news: whatever has been learned can
> be unlearned.[6]

What do you think of these soothing words of "good
news"? Were you created "a warm, caring, outgoing person"? I
wasn't. Is your basic problem only that you "picked up" the
bad habit of relational inadequacy as you have meandered
through life? That's not my basic problem. My basic problem
is best described by these words:

> At one time we too were foolish, disobedient,
> deceived and enslaved by all kinds of passions and

pleasures. We lived in malice and envy, being hated
and hating one another (Titus 3:3).

Does that sound like someone "created [to be] a warm, caring,
outgoing person" who has picked up a bad habit here and
there? Does "Christian" psychology really believe in the biblical doctrine of a sinful nature? If so, why does it continue to
speak that way?

Because they focus so much on people as victims struggling with unmet needs and crippled self-esteem, many
Christian psychologists offer a gospel that won't make people
feel bad about themselves or offend them by exposing their
wickedness and worthlessness (Romans 3:12ff). Their gospel
is all sympathy and little judgment, all love and no wrath, a
gospel with a cross that slightly frowns and gently chides us
into the kingdom. Their gospel never radically offends us or
angers us with its crucified Lord nor warns of God's impending wrath upon impenitent sinners (Luke 13:1-5).

## The Sinner in Scripture

One might truly wish the Bible had such a thoughtful
attitude toward man-the-sinner. The fact is, the Bible is anything but gentle and smiling in its depiction of the sinner's
character and mind-set. Scripture clearly states that from
birth man goes astray (Psalm 58:3) and that "every inclina-
tion of his heart is evil from childhood" (Genesis 8:21). He is
compared to the "tossing sea, which cannot rest" but is constantly churning "up mire and mud" (Isaiah 57:20). His every
good work is a filthy rag in God's sight (Isaiah 64:6) and his
heart is described as "deceitful above all things and beyond
cure" (Jeremiah 17:9).

Scripture also says that man loves to show off his vileness
(Psalm 12:8); that he preys upon the weak (Psalm 10:2-5);
that he loves his sin, is deceitful in conversation and constantly plots evil (Psalm 36:2-4); and that he cannot even
remember how to blush (Jeremiah 6:15). Not a very value-

enhancing portrait, is it? And this is just a small sampling from the Old Testament.

When we turn to the pages of the New Testament, the portrait is uglier, if that is possible. Man's heart is depicted as harboring every evil imaginable (Mark 7:21-23). John's Gospel tells us that man is a slave to sin (8:34) and a child of the devil (8:44). Such words do not exactly give the impression one is simply prone to bad habits.

Romans tells us that man suppresses the clear truth about God (1:18), exchanges that truth for a lie and exchanges God's glory for self-glory (1:22,23). We read that man is filled with and willingly pursues degrading, sexually impure practices (1:24,26). We find he is perverted (1:27), has a depraved mind (1:28), does not seek God willingly (3:11), and is worthless (i.e., useless to God), deceitful, filled with cursing and bitterness, and murderous. Ruin and misery are the chief products of his life (3:12-17).

New Testament Scripture stacks ugly adjective upon ugly adjective, as if hoping to drive us all to a hopeless despair that will cause us "to fear and loathe" sin, in the words of Joseph Alleine, and to charge our "hearts home with these things till it blush for shame, and be brought out of all good opinion of itself."[7]

Scripture depicts man, in his basic character, as well as in his mind-set, as his Creator's implacable and hostile foe. His rebellion has led him into a wicked and wretchedly degrading life style. (See 2 Timothy 3:2-5.)

It is a life style in which man-the-sinner reviles God and mocks His patience and justice (Psalm 10:11,13). It is a life style that creates in man's heart of hearts an insatiable desire to exalt himself above God (Isaiah 14:12-14; Revelation 9:20,21). It is a life style in which he has purposely decided that knowledge of God is not worth retaining (Romans 1:28). And it is a life style that creates in him a rage against God, a lust to be free from all possible divine authority. Willingly, then, man-the-sinner crucifies the Lord of Glory and mocks Him as He hangs compassionately between earth and sky (Mark 15:23-32). Willingly he tramples under foot the Son of

God, treating as "an unholy thing" the only blood of the only covenant that will ever be able to make man acceptable to God (Hebrews 10:29).

This is the biblical view of man outside Christ. It does not allow us to rest comfortably with our self-image. We instinctively cringe before such a naked exposure.

Of course, man is not what God intended him to be when God first created him. His situation is desperate, he is under wrath, he is going to hell, he is unaware of his plight, and he needs to be rescued. This must be brought to the forefront of our thoughts and kept there. This is essential in light of the fact that "Christian" psychology presumes to speak of man from a pathological perspective that says, "Behold, man-the-victim."

The key issue is this. What is the state of man's heart outside Christ? How does the Holy Spirit describe it? This must be our starting and ending point.

"Christian" psychology speaks of victimization; God speaks of the implacable enmity of the wicked toward God. "Christian" psychology speaks of man's painful disappointments and hurts; God speaks of mean-spirited profligates. "Christian" psychology speaks of low self-esteem and the need for appropriate self-love; God speaks of the despicable idolatry of self-worship.

Jesus Christ came into the world to save sinners—no one else. This is the only Gospel there is to preach. Jesus Christ only came into the world to save sinners. Let us not hide the essential. We must not bring people to the cross for the wrong reason or with a wrong understanding. Christ Jesus came into the world to save sinners—of whom I am the worst. Period. None of us is driven into sin reluctantly or against our will. We do not sin merely because we are not loved properly, or our needs are unfulfilled, or we have low self-esteem, or even because we were victimized by our parents or friends or foes. We sin because we are born sinners and delight in sinning, even though such behavior brings terrible consequences upon us all.

I stress the above because many Christians, deeply influenced by psychology, are dangerously close to believing that man's "victimized past" is more responsible for his sinful behavior and his estranged relation with God than is his wicked heart. Those so influenced may **say** that man is a sinner with a sin nature, but the way they evaluate and "treat" man's behavior puts doubt in their confession. So deeply ingrained is the victimization concept in the mind-set of "Christian" psychology that it has altered its understanding of the message of the cross.

Let me illustrate this point. In *Healing for Adult Children of Alcoholics*, Sara Hines Martin, a Christian psychologist, offers a nonscriptural reason for people rejecting Christ, for justifiably turning their backs on the Gospel proclamation and for excusing themselves from any accountability. It is a reason based solely upon their victimization. Her idea radically alters man-the-sinner's culpability before the cross. She writes:

> Recently I heard a sermon entitled, "Why People Reject Jesus." That pastor evidently did not know much about the relationship between abusive fathers and their effects on children because one important reason did not appear on his list; some fathers give such a negative view of God that the children resist any approach to receive Jesus.[8]

Martin maintains that children primarily develop their view of God, at least at the "feeling level" from their human fathers. She insists if that view is bad, those children will reject God and His Son. She then quotes with approval the following words of William De Artago, whom she calls a "specialist in inner healing of memories." He writes:

> When a person is injured by the father, his ability to relate to God is impaired. If his primal image of the father is one that is hurtful, his ability to view God in a healthy way is fractured.[9]

Now, all of this may sound very wise and reasonable, but it is at absolute odds with Scripture. Throughout the whole chapter, Martin never offers one Scripture in support of her thesis. One has to wonder if she really understands the theological implications of her own statements.

However, she does illustrate one vital point in this discussion. When one constantly views the world through a "victimization" grid, the scriptural emphasis on the magnitude of our sin and the necessity of the cross moves more and more into the background. The greater the victimization, the less impelling is the cross.

Let's take a moment to evaluate Martin's comments by Scripture. Is it possible for one outside of Christ to look favorably or "in a healthy way" upon God, considering such Scriptures as Romans 8:6-8? (These verses tell us that the unregenerate mind is hostile to God, unwilling to obey God and unwilling to please Him.) The answer has to be, "No." If we could change our opinion of God through self-effort, then grace would no longer be grace.

Scripture never teaches that one's upbringing is a reason we accept or reject Christ. John 3:19 tells us that "men love darkness instead of light," and Titus 3:3 says they live "in malice and envy, being hated and hating one another." Coupled with Paul's comments in Romans 8:6-8, these verses make Martin's statement dangerous and impossible. It is not our environment that makes Christ and His work desirable, but the Holy Spirit (John 16:7-11). Those who refuse to hear and believe the Gospel are lying if they claim they do so because of the way they were raised. Rather, they do so because in the core of their being they hate God and worship themselves.

Peter did not stand up on the day of Pentecost and offer a twelve-step program to help people get over their aversion to Christ. Paul did not go into Corinth and set up a victimization program. Both preached Jesus Christ and Him crucified, and that "God has made this Jesus, whom you crucified, both Lord and Christ" (Acts 2:36). To imply that people can understandably reject Christ because they were raised in homes where the father was a "sinner" who didn't model an acceptable picture of God is simply not biblical Christianity.

Will anyone avoid judgment for such a reason? Are we not by nature "objects of wrath" (Ephesians 2:3)? Will anyone stand before the throne of God and blame Him for giving them an earthly father who made it difficult for them to believe in God and His Christ? For men to make excuses to avoid the cross is not new. For "Christian" psychology to justify these excuses on the grounds of victimization is extremely disturbing. It is evident that constant emphasis on victimization is making it difficult for us to see our own sinfulness with the dreadful seriousness God demands.

The next story will bear this out. The above example showed how victimization allows us to "legitimately" avoid the cross. The following example will show how victimization, not personal sin, is a greater reason for coming to the cross.

A young South American had a reputation as a macho playboy, but this was all surface. Inside, the young man was filled with deep emotional pain because he had been homosexually abused as a child. He was enslaved and tormented by vile memories. This childhood abuse led him into a life "of drugs, drinking and immorality—all efforts to prove that [he] was a man."[10]

One day some missionaries moved into the young man's neighborhood. Though he claimed to despise them, much to his surprise he accepted their invitation to attend a Christian camp. At the camp, away from alcohol and drugs, he had a great time and many of the young people described their relationship with Jesus. They told him that "Jesus died for the wrong things [he] had done and all [he] had to do for God to accept [him] was to trust Him to forgive [him]."

The young man didn't understand it all but he began to believe that maybe it was true. Romans 8:38-39 deeply moved him. "Somehow," he said, "I knew that not even sexual abuse and a seemingly ruined life could stop God from loving me." On the last night of camp he told God, "My life has been all messed up. If you really are alive and can live in someone like this, then come into my life and change it. I need you."

When the young man returned home he went through many ups and downs as he sought to live out his new found faith. But he "knew God wanted [him] to go straight," so he did. As his knowledge of God grew, his walk became more consistent and he hungered to know the Scriptures better. To pursue this goal he came to America and ended up at Moody Bible Institute. At the close of his testimony, he included these words: "The greatest struggle of my life has finally been eradicated: no longer am I plagued by painful memories of abuse."

"For by His wounds we were healed." Too many believers fail to appropriate this marvelous truth. I thank God that this young man is a joint heir in Christ. But his testimony clearly illustrates the subtle way that "Christian" psychology is altering how we are responding to the message of the cross. What bothers me most is that his testimony lacks a deep sense of personal sinfulness. What is stressed instead is his victimization as a child. He held his abuse responsible for his life of immorality, drugs and meanness, and even his personality traits. His awareness that God loved him "anyway" was centered in his abuse and his "ruined life"—not from any deep sense of conviction over his own sin. We learn that the greatest struggle of his life was not over guilt from personal sin, but rather the painful memories of his abuse.

Do not misunderstand. I do not wish to belittle the pain of this young man's terrible childhood. Nor deny that it impacted his life adversely. Nor do I expect a new convert to understand fully the doctrine of sin before he can trust Christ as his Lord and Savior. Still, one cannot help but sense that his understanding of the cross has been influenced by psychology with its emphasis on victimization. His story is not a clear declaration that "Christ Jesus came into the world to save sinners—of whom I am the worst" (1 Timothy 1:15). Rather, his story seems to read, "Christ Jesus has come into the world to meet the needs of those who have been victimized, whose lives have been messed up by victimization—and I am among the most victimized."

How far removed that is from the testimony of another sinner, Tokichi Ichii. Ichii was a convicted felon who was hanged for murder in Tokyo in 1918. Shortly before he was sentenced to death, he was given a New Testament. Soon thereafter two woman missionaries visited him and helped guide him in his study of Scripture. After reading about Jesus' trial and crucifixion, he trusted Christ as his Lord and Savior. He had been exceptionally cruel and brutal and incorrigible before his conversion. Now that he was in Christ he accepted his death sentence as "the fair, impartial judgment of God."

As his execution approached, he read 2 Corinthians 6:8-10 and he wrote that though people might think him in distress, such was not the case. He was "infinitely happier" in his tiny prison cell than he had been "in the days of [his] sinning when [he] did not know God." He wrote, "Day and night . . . I am talking with Jesus Christ."

The words "poor, yet making many rich" in those verses caught his attention and he wrote:

> This certainly does not apply to the evil life I led before I repented. But perhaps in the future, someone in the world may hear that the most desperate villain that ever lived repented of his sins and was saved by the power of Christ, and so may come to repent also. Then it may be that though I am poor myself, I shall be able to make many rich.[11]

Tokichi Ichii lived before Christians learned they must become victim conscious. Thus the full weight of his sin was not lightened by thoughts of having been victimized by others. Again, let me say I do not mean to belittle the young South American's sexually abused childhood. Those who so abuse children give gruesome evidence that man's heart is indeed desperately wicked. But this is the issue we must not lose sight of: **my** sinfulness is the only issue I must deal with at the cross. Had this young man never been molested, he would have still grown up twisted by sin and given over to delighting in wickedness. The fact of abuse doesn't change the fact that outside Christ he was first and foremost a lover of self rather than a lover of God. It is this that God wants us to understand. It is this God wants us to mourn over as we approach the cross.

Sin is not a virus we catch from someone else. Nor is it a character role imposed upon us by outside forces. It is our very nature outside Christ. By acting wickedly before God, we are only being ourselves. We cannot avoid responsibility for our sin, even if others have treated us badly. One does not come to Christ complaining that others have forced us to become sinners against our will.

Unless we take sin and our resulting worthlessness seriously, we will not take the cross seriously. If we will not take sin seriously, neither will we take seriously our forgiveness nor respond to God with obedient and profound love (Luke 7:41ff). Failure to take sin seriously will weaken every other aspect of our understanding and worship of God.

## Understanding God's Love

Perhaps you are thinking that in my zeal for a proper understanding and acceptance of our sin, I obscure the wondrous love and tender compassions of God. That I make Him seem unmoved and uncaring toward the terrible miseries which so often attend our way. Misery and unhappiness often come upon us without any immediate blame on our part. Surely in such moments God cares about us and is with us.

"God is love." That is true. Such is the primary message of the Scriptures. But if, as John writes, "This is love: not that we loved God, but that He loved us and sent His Son as an atoning sacrifice for our sins" (1 John 4:10), then I must proclaim it to others from that context. Can I speak of God's love and say nothing about our need to repent? Can I say, "God is love," and never mention His Holiness? Shall I extol His mercy and be mute about His wrath? Dare I say anyone on earth deserves God's love due to their circumstances? Does this take sin seriously? The cup of God's love is offered only to those who mourn over their sin (Matthew 5:4).

While we were yet enemies, God loved us. Jesus Christ delivered Himself up for me long before I ceased relishing every opportunity to blaspheme Him. That makes His love all the more amazing. Indeed, it is only God's transforming love that can turn the curse into praise, the blasphemer into the worshiper, the wicked heart into the adoring heart.

Until that happens, it is also true that in His holy soul God hates the wicked and wrongdoer (Psalm 11:5 and 5:5). He declares sinners without excuse for their sinful attitudes and behavior (Romans 1:20). He has given them over to the consequences of their sin in this life (Romans 1:24) and deprived them of any inheritance in the one to come (Ephesians 5:5). By their very nature, God has declared them to be objects of wrath (Ephesians 2:3), storing up all their lives more and more wrath for the day of His wrath (Romans 2:5).

This is the context in which God's love is to be understood and proclaimed. Amazing and undeserved! We must not deny God's holiness and our unholiness when we talk of His love. It is a grievous wrong to lead unconverted sinners to believe that God is with them in their "pain and disappointments" in an intimate and personal way, such as He is with the believer, when they are still in rebellion against the cross. He is not! He wants to be—that is why He sent His Son to die on the cross—but He is not.

We cannot benefit from God's love until we come to the cross, not in hostility or self-pity or resentment, but only in broken-hearted repentance. Then, and only then, is God free to pour His affections out upon us in unlimited portions (1 John 3:1). I treasure the manner in which the Puritan William Bridges expressed it: "If you lay yourself at Christ's feet, He will take you in His arms."[12]

We can only preach Jesus Christ and Him crucified. This is the only Gospel of God's love. It is a message for sinners, not victims. It is a message for predators, not the preyed upon. If all I need from God is sympathy and compassion because I am hurt and disappointed and betrayed, and my self-esteem has been damaged, Christ need not have died. Sinners, on the other hand, desperately need the cross. They need forgiveness and there is no forgiveness without the shedding of blood, specifically the blood of Christ (Hebrews 9:22-28).

We only have the commission to preach the Gospel God has given us in His Word. We must preach it unadorned by all the psychological modifications we are attaching to it. We must return to the clear proclamation of the Scriptures. We must preach the Gospel given to us once for all or we deny its authority as well as its sufficiency. "Christ Jesus came into the world to save sinners—of whom I am the worst." This is why God's love in Christ is so amazing, so astounding, so humbling and so liberating.

---

## Notes

1   Philip P. Bliss, "Hallelujah! What a Saviour."

2   Joseph Alleine, *An Alarm to Unconverted Sinners* (Grand Rapids: Baker Book House, 1978), p. 112. This book is also available under the title *A Sure Guide to Heaven*.

3        This theme of betrayal or "victimization" seems paramount for "Christian" psychology. Believers must feel deeply the pain of their victimization or they will never be free from its bondage or their own sinful responses. Attempts to justify this idea scripturally lead to some awkward interpretations of Bible stories. One example of this is a Christian counselor who had a junior high girls' Sunday school class deeply identify with the feelings of betrayal Mary supposedly experienced when she learned that Joseph was going to cancel their marriage.

There are at least two serious difficulties with this interpretation. First, we don't know how Joseph found out about Mary's pregnancy, nor do we have any information that Joseph discussed his plan with Mary. The account in Matthew 1:18-24 is too sketchy to draw the kind of conclusion the Christian counselor drew.

All we know is that Joseph did not realize that Mary's pregnancy was of the Holy Spirit until the Lord revealed it to him in a dream. We do not know if he ever spoke with Mary or told her he was terminating the marriage.

Matthew's account also makes it difficult to accuse Joseph of betraying Mary. In fact, he showed a great deal of tenderness and consideration toward Mary. He did not want her to be hurt or shamed by public ridicule. If anyone had a right to "feel" betrayed at first, it was Joseph. But we don't read of Joseph being absorbed in Joseph. Rather, he was concerned for Mary.

Second, anyone who reads Mary's song in Luke 1:46-56 will have a hard time believing it reflects a young woman filled with feelings of fear, rejection and betrayal. She is absolutely humbled and at the same time filled with a glorious joy that God had chosen her to bear the promised Messiah. Mary praises God and rejoices in Him because "the Mighty one has done great things for me— holy is his name" (Luke 1:46-49).

Whatever the immediate consequences of her pregnancy on others, Mary does not seem apprehensive about it. God had spoken to Mary through Gabriel and Elizabeth. Mary knew and trusted her God. That was more than enough for Mary's emotional well-being.

This incident shows the problem with "Christian" psychology's victimization approach to Scripture and life. First, trying to force its assumptions onto Scripture, it skews a legitimate interpretation. In using the Mary/Joseph story to validate its teachings about betrayal, Scripture is badly misused.

"Christian" psychology simply cannot integrate the impact an intimate relationship with God has upon the way a believer responds to the "hurts and disappointments" of life. Psychology says Mary had to feel betrayed because that is the way it "reads" people. But Scripture indicates Mary was filled with joy and trusted herself to God.

4    "Religious Belief vs. Behavior," *The Church Around the World* (September, 1989).

5    Ann Landers, "Beware the Wolf in Minister's Clothing" (*The Los Angeles Times*, August 17, 1989), p. 25.

6    The ad appeared on p. 28 of *Christianity Today* (September 8, 1989). The book is titled *Friendship*, published by Zondervan.

7    Alleine, *op. cit.* p. 132.

8    Sara Hines Martin, *Healing for Adult Children of Alcoholics* (Nashville: Broadman Press, 1988), p. 135.

9    *Ibid.*, p. 135.

10   Manuel Zarate as told to Wendy Cameron, "First Person," *Moody Monthly* (September 1989), p. 80.

11   Tokichi Ichii's testimony is related in John Piper's *Desiring God* (Portland: Multnomah Press, 1986), pp. 120, 121.

12   *The Golden Treasury of Puritan Quotations*, compiled by I.D.E. Thomas (Chicago: Moody Press, 1975), p. 149.

# 3

# Off and Running
# with Self-Esteem

If ever there was a word that could cast a spell of
enchantment over the eyes of the evangelical community,
*self-esteem* is that word. And cast a spell it has. Perhaps it
was inevitable, considering "Christian" psychology's preoccupation with pathological man. The result is that preoccupation with self-esteem has become the norm for far too many
Christians—a condition that is less than inspiring. So let us
focus for a bit on the Christian and his or her self-esteem.

However, before I begin my analysis, let me take a few
paragraphs to make sure we both understand the situation. I
want to be careful here; I don't want to beat the air or box
with shadows.

First, most Christian psychologists are one with most secular psychologists in embracing the idea that a person's opinion of himself—that is, his level of self-esteem or self-worth or
self-love—determines how well that person will function and
what kind of contribution he or she will make in life.

Second, most Christian psychologists accept, as do most
secular psychologists, the premise that low self esteem is the
cause of most human behavioral problems. The state of California appointed a commission that spent $735,000 unsuc-

cessfully trying to verify this very thing. Is one sexually promiscuous, abusive, abused, codependent, taking drugs, pushing drugs, having marriage problems or just feeling generally inferior? You name it and low self-esteem will claim it.[1]

Third, "Christian" psychology agrees with secular psychology's unproven assumptions that practically everyone suffers from low self-esteem. Parents, other family members, strangers, society as a whole, and the world in general all supposedly contribute to robbing us of a proper sense of self-worth. I remember a comic strip in which one cartoon character blamed his ill treatment of another character on a "victimization disorder" caused by his pet dog beating him up.

## Self-Worth Invades the Church

Magazines and newspapers, TV and radio programs, seminars and books without number drum this so-called truth into our minds—including, now, the Christian media and publishers. Self-worth is one of the most potent humanistic ideas to invade the church in this century. It is one of the most serious challenges to the Scriptures in recent memory. Of all the areas in which Scripture can be wrongly used, supporting self-esteem is near the top of the list.

A few years ago, I was attempting to recruit students for college outreach ministries. Some students excused themselves by saying they didn't yet love themselves the way they needed to. If they didn't love themselves the way they ought to, they wondered how could they love others in obedience to the biblical command?

Where on earth did they get such an outlandish interpretation of the second commandment? I soon discovered they learned it from a Christian psychologist who was teaching the general education psychology course. Using Matthew 22:39 ("love your neighbor as yourself"), he had convinced many students that Christ was commanding us to love ourselves before we could love our neighbor.

The wonder is that just such an interpretation, founded on horrible exegesis, is being enthusiastically embraced by a growing segment of the evangelical church. This ought to cause alarm bells to sound all over. Unfortunately, in too many cases, there is only silence.

It makes me wonder: will an authoritative Scripture, properly exegeted, continue to mean anything to evangelicals? If so, we must take a close and critical look at this teaching on self-love. Is it scriptural? Let's begin with Matthew 22:39 and work to a conclusion from there.

### How Are We To Love Ourselves?

Matthew 22:39 reads, "And the second is like the first [commandment]: 'love your neighbor as yourself.' " It sounds straightforward, doesn't it? We needn't spend much time deciding whether Christ is instructing us to love ourselves first. If He wanted to make that the main thrust of this commandment, He would have made it clear. I can imagine Him saying something like, "You need to love yourself, and when you have learned to do that, then love your neighbor in the same way." But He didn't!

What He said was, "Love your neighbor as yourself." The Lord knew that self-love already exists in generous amounts. The fact that Christ compares it to the First Commandment, the thrust of the sentence itself (our neighbor's need), and the use of the verb *agapao* (which speaks of other-directed love) all mitigate against the idea that Christ is telling us to learn to love ourselves first.[2] To interpret Christ's commandment to love others as a command to love ourselves is to openly ignore the intent of God's Word.[3]

In one of his latest books, *Healing Grace*, David Seamands is willing to concede that "it is technically true to say that we are not actually commanded in these Scriptures to love ourselves." But then he claims Scripture assumes we have a healthy self-love, a proper sense of self-worth, and thus are able to respond to Christ's command in an appropriate way.[4]

Unfortunately, psychology says, we all know that most people have a very poor self-image and some even hate themselves. These folks need to learn to love themselves before they can biblically love others (and, one assumes, God).

What an interesting bit of maneuvering! The reasoning goes something like this: we can't give what we don't have. If one doesn't appreciate one's own worth and significance, then one cannot give to others the love they need to make them feel worthwhile and significant. If one is "dysfunctional" because of a low self-esteem, how can one help another who is also "dysfunctional" for the same reason? Thus the need to love ourselves.

The material flowing from the pens of Christian psychologists in this regard is voluminous. It might be profitable, then, to review one of these apologies for self-love in order to clearly grasp the implications of integrating it with Scripture. Is learning to love ourselves a biblical mandate?

Psychologist Raymond Chester believes it is and he has written a self-study booklet, *Do I Really Have Value? A Study in Self-Love*, to help us come to the same conclusion.[5] Dr. Chester's booklet is typical of the material "Christian" psychology is publishing on self-love. It does have the wonderful advantage of being brief.

Most Christians, Chester believes, consider anything smacking of self to be a sin. He disagrees. He believes an appropriate self-love appreciates the value one has because one is made in God's image. (This is often called our "created value.") Self-esteem results from our recognition of this fact and is rooted in God's love for us.

Dr. Chester also believes "few Christians know how to biblically love themselves," because most believers don't know who they are. This limits their ability to understand who others are and hampers them from truly loving others and ministering to them properly.[6] The booklet was written to help answer the question, "Who am I?" and from the answer discover a positive (and biblical) sense of self-worth. Then, presumably, the reader will be able to help others discover their biblical value. But, the Bible never centers on self-understanding of one's worth as a prerequisite for loving others in obedience to Christ's command. Rather, Christ predicates our obedience on our love for Him and an appreciation of how much He loves us (John 13:34 and 14:15).

Using a series of fill-in exercises, combined with encouraging evaluations drawn from what Dr. Chester sees as self-value-enhancing verses, the participant is guided into discovering his identity and true worth. The last exercise is to be "an affirmation statement of 'who I am,' " in light of God's true view of me.

Dr. Chester hopes that we have all "been a part of helping someone else discover that they too have self-worth—and not because of you or me, but because of Christ . . . How much more worth could anyone want . . . *I am,*" Dr. Chester boldly proclaims, "*because He is!*"[7] (Emphasis his.)

Interestingly, Dr. Chester also includes in his booklet—verbatim—a short essay "from a secular source." The essay is titled "My Declaration of Self-Esteem" and is written by Virginia Satir, a secular humanist.[8] Let me summarize it, for while I find it a fascinating statement on human self-love, I am shocked that it should be integrated into a Christian study on self-worth supposedly grounded in Scripture.

Satir's essay is an exercise in self-exaltation. She owns herself and "everything about me," as she puts it. Whatever she says, thinks, does, or feels at any moment is the authentic Virginia. If she finds something unfitting or unbecoming in who she is, she believes she can discard it and "invent something new for that which [she] discarded." Supremely self-confident concerning her identity and her abilities to negotiate the highs and lows of being human, Satir concludes by writing, "I own me, and therefore I can engineer me. I am me, and I am okay."

At the conclusion of this essay, Dr. Chester encourages us to:

> . . . prayerfully integrate this knowledge of who you are into your everyday life (work, home, play, etc.). As a person of worth and quality you can truly "do

everything . . . heartily, as for the Lord rather than for men" (Colossians 3:23).[9]

Considering the nature of Satir's essay, this is an odd request—one I want to return to shortly. But first let us turn to the Scriptures.

## The Bible and Self-Esteem

Despite "Christian" psychology's insistence that we must learn to love ourselves, it is difficult, when one considers the biblical depiction of man-the-sinner, to discover someone who doesn't already love himself excessively. For example, Psalm 10 describes man as arrogant, boastful, haughty and pleased with himself. In reading Romans 1:18-32, one gets the overwhelming impression of a race of beings bursting with self-love and self-worth.

The same picture emerges in 2 Timothy 3:1-5. In that passage Paul warns of what people will be like in the "last days." Among other things, they are described as "lovers of themselves, boastful, proud [and] conceited."

In an unintended way, Dr. Seamands is right. Scripture does assume we love ourselves. But Scripture does not assume (with the exception given in Ephesians 5:28,29 where a natural desire for physical and mental well-being is normal) that our self-love is appropriate, proper, or God-approved. Scripture assumes we love ourselves because it is the unavoidable expression of our sin nature. By nature we love ourselves above all things, including and especially God.

There is a tragic sorrow in Christ relating to us the two great commandments, for we cannot obey either one. The reason we cannot obey is not because we do not love ourselves enough, but rather the opposite. We love ourselves too much—so much so that we cannot begin to love another with the same intensity.

Only in Christ are we redeemed from this self-idolatry. For "Christian" psychology to tell us we need to learn to love ourselves properly is to set itself at cross-purposes with what our Lord Jesus teaches. His example of servanthood should encourage us to relinquish our sinful drive to exalt ourselves.

Let's look at a couple of vignettes from Scripture, which show how God values those who self-consciously hold "appropriate" self-esteem and those who have a "wretched" self-image.

Luke 7:36-50 tells the story of Simon and the sinful woman. Simon was a self-confident man who loved himself so robustly that he had no trouble even putting down Jesus. He felt good about himself. Yet his very self-esteem, based upon his perceived relationship with God, had led him into an insensitivity to his own sinfulness that left him alienated from his Messiah.

The sinful woman, on the other hand, had only a wretched view of herself. She fully realized her sinfulness. Yet she did not come to Christ as one abused and robbed of a proper sense of self-worth. Rather, she came to Christ as one knowing He had come into the world to save sinners, of whom she was among the worst. She came seeking mercy and forgiveness—and she received them. I doubt she left thinking how good she could now feel about herself. Rather, she left with a sense of overwhelming gratitude and a love for Christ that humbled her, that compelled her to become a willing servant and follower.

A similar scenario is presented in Luke 18:9-14. It is the parable of the Pharisee and the Tax Collector. The Pharisee was confident in his relationship with God and exuded a wonderful sense of self-worth. One cannot help thinking the Pharisee believed his relationship with God gave him reason to feel special. Yet this very relational confidence placed him far from God.

On the other hand, like the prostitute, the Tax Collector was devastated by his awareness of what a wretched sinner he was before a holy and righteous God. Knowing well he did not deserve it, he pleaded mercy from God, But I suspect he knew what God had promised in the Scriptures—that He would not despise "a broken and contrite heart" (Psalm

51:17). God, in His unfathomable grace, not only dwelt in "a high and holy place but also with him who is contrite and lowly in spirit, to revive the spirit of the lowly and revive the heart of the contrite" (Isaiah 57:15).

People who have truly experienced the richness of God's undeserved mercy in Christ are not concerned with whether they have "appropriate" self-love. Rather, there flows from their hearts these words: "To God be the glory, great things He has done!"

## Great Saints and Self-Esteem

It might also be valuable to reflect on how some of the great saints of the Bible viewed themselves in light of their relationship with God. Did they consciously affirm to themselves an appropriate sense of self-worth because God loved them? Let us see.

Abraham, the friend of God, called himself "nothing but dust and ashes" in the presence of the Lord (Genesis 18:27). Moses, with whom God spoke face to face, begged God to send someone else to lead, because he did not consider himself capable to do so, even with God's assistance (Exodus 4). God praised Job, but when God confronted him, Job declared, "Therefore I despise myself and repent in dust and ashes" (Job 42:6). In Psalm 51, David, a man after God's own heart, pleads for God's forgiveness and restoration of fellowship, admitting that his sin was always before him. Yet he clings to this knowledge: "The sacrifices of God are a broken spirit; a broken and contrite heart, O God, you will not despise" (verse 17). Isaiah, starkly aware of his own sinfulness, could only pronounce his own condemnation when he saw God in all His holiness (Isaiah 6:5).

The Apostle John, a special recipient of Jesus' love among the Twelve, "fell at his feet as though dead" when he saw Jesus in His true ascension glory (Revelation 1:12-17). The Apostle Paul named himself the foremost of sinners who received, not only undeserved grace from the Lord, but a satanic tormentor as well, to make sure he would not become conceited. He consistently spoke of his absolute dependence on Christ's power and grace (2 Corinthians 12:7-10). All his desires and ambitions focused on one thing: "to know Christ and the power of his resurrection and the fellowship of sharing in his suffering, becoming like him in his death" (Philippians 3:10). To tell himself he could now love himself in Christ seems the furthest thought from his mind.

None of these men seemed concerned about their self-worth. I doubt any of them would have declared with Dr. Chester, "I am because He is!" to justify self-consciously loving themselves. I doubt they would have clamored to participate in his study. Far more important to them were these words of their Lord: "This is the one I esteem: he who is humble and contrite in spirit and trembles at my word" (Isaiah 66:2).

These biblical saints would have little in common with Dr. Chester or a host of present-day Christian psychologists who insist we need to "biblically" love ourselves more. On the other hand, they would have a great deal in common with the father of modern missions, William Carey, who asked that these words be inscribed upon his tombstone:

> William Carey
> Born August 17th, 1761
> Died June 1834
> A wretched, poor and helpless worm,
> on Thy kind arms I fall.

This man accomplished tremendous things with his "worm mentality"—all by the grace of God.

## Which Direction?

The issue is this. Which direction are we to face? Where are my eyes to rest? Were these Scriptures, now used as a green light for proclaiming self-worth, really given to us for that purpose? Or were they written to rivet our attention on the all-surpassing wonder of God's grace and, at the same time, increase our confidence in His faithfulness, that we might learn to esteem Him above all else and to feel good about Him?

To use such Scriptures—meant to focus us on God's great worth and value, His majesty, awesomeness, omnipotence and faithfulness, and designed to create in us an uncontainable sense of joy and reverent worship—to focus on me and give myself permission to build up my self-esteem is inappropriate, even ungodly. It is completely against the intent of the Holy Spirit in giving them to us.

What is lacking in all those who insist we have "appropriate" self-love before we can truly obey the second commandment is an understanding of what it means to be a new creation in Christ (2 Corinthians 5:16,17). Only Christ frees us from that natural compulsion to worship ourselves.

As a result of having been made new in Christ through faith in His finished work upon the cross, every believer has the ability to keep this commandment because:

1. God's love is of such a nature that we cannot contain it. "God has poured out his love into our hearts by the Holy Spirit whom he has given us" (Romans 5:5). John tells us He has lavished His great love upon us (1 John 3:1). It fills up our lives and spills over into the lives of others. I appreciate the way John Piper expresses it: "Love is the overflow of joy in God that gladly meets the needs of others."[10]

2. He has taught us both what love is and how we are to express it. (See 1 John 3:16-18; 4:7-11; and Philippians 2:5-8.) He gave His life that we might have life; He traded His kingly crown for a servant's sweatband. He did not worry about His self-esteem, His acceptance by others, His comfort or His influence. He simply served and served right up to the cross and into the tomb. His Father highly exalted Him for doing this.

3. When we are indwelt by the Holy Spirit, it is Christ's love that compels us and makes us able to (a) no longer live for ourselves but completely for Him (2 Corinthians 5:14,15);

(b) be ambassadors for Him, sharing with the world the goods news of the sinner's reconciliation with God through Christ (2 Corinthians 5:20); and (c) continue to pay the debt of love we owe all men, "for he who loves his fellowman has fulfilled the law" (Romans 13:8-10).

It is no longer our love as such that we share with our neighbor, but the love that Christ has given us. His love flows from Him into us and out of us to others. Thus, its expression needn't wait for me to develop "appropriate, biblical self-love." Paul reminds us that we hold "this treasure in jars of clay" [a designation we are to glory in], so that all might understand who it is who makes this possible, "to show that this all surpassing power is from God and not from us" (2 Corinthians 4:7).

Loving my neighbor has nothing to do with my self-esteem and everything to do with Christ Jesus our Lord. The second commandment can only be understood in conjunction with the undeserved love God the Father showered upon us when we were placed into Christ by the Holy Spirit. It can only be practiced by the Christian as he abides in Christ and as Christ and His Word abide in him (John 15:4-7).

Dr. Chester's booklet on self-worth had us study Psalm 139 for the explicit purpose of instilling in us "appropriate" self-love. But was that the intent of the Holy Spirit when He inspired this psalm? This psalm speaks in awesome tones of the omnipotence, omniscience, and omnipresence of the Lord of Glory. Doesn't it seem strange that we should put such Scripture as this to the task of building our self-esteem?

For fairness' sake, Dr. Chester might have constructed an exercise that asks us why God should hold us so precious. Sin stands between God and me, not ignorance of my created value. God is not obligated to redeem me because He created me. But He has obligated Himself to love me if I am in Christ. Why? Because He said He would.

## Why Does God Love Us?

Jesus Christ. Those are the only two words I can think of to explain why God holds me dear. Or, as Paul wrote to the Ephesians:

> Praise be to the God and Father of our Lord Jesus Christ, who has blessed us in the heavenly realms with every spiritual blessing in Christ. For he chose us in him before the creation of the world to be holy and blameless in his sight. In love he predestined us to be adopted as his sons through Jesus Christ, in accordance with his pleasure and will—to the praise of his glorious grace, which he has freely given us in the one he loves. In him we have redemption through his blood, the forgiveness of sins, in accordance with the riches of God's grace that he lavished on us with all wisdom and understanding (Ephesians 1:3-8).

In light of these verses, what compels "Christian" psychology to be so concerned with stroking our esteem? Why is it so preoccupied with self-absorbed propositions?

The question becomes especially pertinent when we consider Dr. Chester's use of the secular "My Declaration of Self-Esteem," a work that merely restates William Henley's 19th century "Invictus." That famous poem strutted forth a lying courage that every rebel against God would like to claim for himself. Do you recall this verse from it?

> It matters not how strait the gate,
> How charged with punishment the scroll,
> I am the master of my fate;
> I am the captain of my soul.

Henley did not consider it necessary to retain a knowledge of God—and neither did the author of "My Declaration of Self-Esteem."

But what has Jerusalem to do with Athens? What has Virginia Satir in common with Jesus Christ? What have the words, "I own me, and therefore I can engineer me. I am me, and I am okay," have in common with the words, "Do you not know that your body is a temple of the Holy Spirit, who is in you, whom you have received from God? You are not your own; you were bought at a price. Therefore honor God with your body" (1 Corinthians 6:19,20)?

How can believers "prayerfully integrate" Satir's self-exalting fantasy into their everyday life in Christ? Surely "Christian" psychology has lost touch with the head if it believes this is advisable!

## A Skewed Focus

There is something bankrupt about an idea that purports to be scripturally grounded yet reinforces itself with such humanistic materials as Satir's essay. The focus on self-esteem by Christian psychologists has little in common with the focus of the cross. Are believers so spiritually deprived and disappointed by being crucified with Christ, for having died and finding their lives now hidden with Christ in God (Colossians 3:3), that they must scamper about from mirror to mirror until they find just the right one to tell them they can "biblically" love themselves? If so, perhaps we ought "to be pitied more than all men" after all.

Is this "integration with Scripture" an example of how we are to apply the "discovered" truths of behavioral science? There is little to admire in any of this, and even less to praise.

Not too long ago, a friend of mine, a children's pastor, reported an interesting event that took place at his church's winter retreat for juniors. On the last night of the retreat the speaker asked the children to think of one thing that would allow them to feel good about themselves. After consulting with their counselors (knowing perhaps it would be unchristian to say "because I am handsome" or "smart" or some such thing), they decided they could feel good about themselves because of John 3:16.

My friend was elated with their choice. But my response was to blurt out, "But that doesn't make any sense!" Had the speaker asked the children why they could have good feelings as believers, I would have had no objections. Believers can certainly feel good because God loves them and sent His Son to die for their sins. They ought to experience joy and peace. They ought to be even more overwhelmed with gratitude toward God, deep feelings of love, and thankfulness.

But both of these "feelings" are a continent apart from saying I feel good about myself because God sent His Son to die on the cross on my behalf—an act of love I did not deserve. The point of John 3:16 is **not** about **my** value, but about God's amazing love, that God is rich in mercy toward those who love darkness.

## The Parable of Heathen

Let me relate a parable. Once there were two neighbors. One was surly, boastful, hateful, immoral and unceasingly self-centered. Let us call him Heathen. The other was kindly, humble, god fearing and always thoughtful toward others. Christian is his name. Because Heathen was such a loutish boor, he was always in trouble or causing trouble for others. Christian was forever reaching out to Heathen with offers of help and encouraging him to live a better life. But Heathen would have none of it. He spurned Christian's every overture of friendship. Worse still, he cursed Christian and slandered him to others in the neighborhood.

"What a meddling, goody-two-shoes fool he is," Heathen would say, loud enough for all to hear, "with his 'churchianity' and his precious Bible verses. They're all hypocrites, you know, and Christian is the worst of the lot." He laughed at Christian's goodness and went out of his way to make life miserable whenever the opportunity presented itself. All of Christian's offers of friendship were spurned and his encouragements for Heathen to mend his ways before his wickedness brought him to ruin fell on deaf ears.

Finally, however, a day came when Christian's warnings proved true. Heathen was viciously set upon by a group of men as vile and wicked as himself. Powerless to escape and helpless to fend off his attackers (he recognized some of them as those he had called friends), he was beaten to the ground and his end seemed deservedly near. Death and hell, snarling gleefully and contemptuous of his pleas for mercy, greedily reached out for their prize. But suddenly Christian was standing over him, fighting off his enemies, displaying a courage and strength Heathen never dreamed Christian possessed.

When the last enemy had fled, Christian turned and gave his attention to Heathen. Ignoring his own wounds, Christian tenderly bandaged Heathen's, staining the dressing with his own blood. Then he gave Heathen a cool drink that refreshed Heathen's soul.

Christian paid dearly for his act of selflessness toward his old enemy, however. His own many wounds were deep and mortal. Scarcely had he raised Heathen to his feet, than he himself collapsed and died on the very spot where Heathen had lain a moment before.

Heathen stared in numbed disbelief. Then he turned—weeping, broken in spirit and humbled in heart as never before—and shamefully retreated into his house. He did not pause until he reached his bedroom. Once there he stood before his wall mirror and surveyed his battered but bandaged reflection. Then he spoke.

"Heathen," he whispered through raw lips, "do you realize what Christian just did for you? Do you realize he saved you and gave his life for you?" He paused, then placed his heels together, sucked in his stomach, pushed out his chest, tucked in his chin and looked straight into his reflected, blood-shot eyes. "Heathen, you have never experienced such undeserved love in all your life. Do you know what, Heathen? I feel good about myself because of it. Yes, now I can have a sense of self-worth and can love myself appropriately because of Christian's gracious sacrifice."

Nonsensical, isn't it? So it is with us, but even more so—vile, wicked sinners, standing at the foot of the cross, washed pure in the blood of the Lamb by God Himself. Oh, see the love of the Father, reconciling Himself to us, not counting our sins against us, even as we nail His Son to the cross and curse His name! Was there ever a more despicable act? Was there ever a greater mercy extended? Shall we now pause, even as we eagerly partake of that mercy, and turn our eyes from the cross to our own reflection and say to ourselves, "Oh, but I feel good about myself because of this"?

How I wish that everyone would see this nonsense for what it is. Then I would not have to write another word. How can any believer say, "Before I can love another, I must first focus on learning to love myself?"

Have we gone mad?

---

## Notes

1    How far have we gone in this regard? Well, consider the following newspaper excerpt:

> Bush's need to move in the mideast came about because of Saddam Hussein. Saddam has a particularly despicable personality, **accompanied by a lack of self-esteem**. (Notice how he rarely appears on public television, but has an announcer with a similar appearance read his speeches). (Bill Thomas, "U.S. Influence Emerging From Persian Gulf War," *The Bakersfield Californian*, March 3, 1991, p. 9, emphasis added.)

2    One only has to read the parable of the Good Samaritan (Luke 10:25-37) to understand exactly what Christ meant when He taught us to love our neighbor as our-

selves. For anyone to turn this into a command for me to learn to love myself first is simply practicing eisegesis, and doing so for self-serving reasons.

3     After I had first written these words, I came across this statement by David Seamands, one of the leaders in the healing memories school of counseling:

> Jesus said that we should love God with our whole hearts and love our neighbors as we love ourselves. Love for self is as necessary for maturity and wholeness and holiness as is love for God and for other people. Indeed, loving God and loving my neighbor requires a measure of self-acceptance and self-love in which I hold my selfhood in esteem, integrity, identity and respect. (David Seamands, *Putting Away Childish Things*, Wheaton: Victor Books, 1982, p. 114.)

4    David A. Seamands, *Healing Grace* (Wheaton: Victor Books, 1988), pp. 141, 142.

5    Raymond H. Chester, *Do I Really Have Value?* (Fresno, CA: Link Care Missions), 1984, p. 1.

6    *Ibid.*, p. 3.

7    *Ibid.*, p. 20.

8    *Ibid.*, p. 22.
    Virginia Satir was one of the pioneers in the self-esteem movement and was a member of the California Task Force to Promote Self-Esteem. In fact, the task force dedicated its final report to her. She died in September, 1988.

9    *Ibid.*, p. 23.

10  John Piper, *Desiring God: Meditations of a Christian Hedonist* (Portland: Multnomah Press, 1986), p. 96.

# 4

# John Stott
# on Self-Esteem

Shakespeare's Juliet had a problem. Although she realized Romeo was the son of her father's bitter enemy, she was unwilling to deny her desire for him. "That which we call a rose," she said, "by any other name, would smell as sweet." But to love Romeo, Juliet had to accept the name and all it symbolized—a decision that proved deadly for both her lover and herself.

So it is with those Christians who realize, deep down, that advocating greater self-love cannot be justified biblically. Yet at the same time, they are so persuaded by psychology of the necessity of developing high self-esteem that they find themselves in an awkward dilemma. How can they keep the one but discard the other? The rose of self-love smells too sweet to cast aside, but they dare not keep the name lest it prove their undoing.

The results are often labored semantics, bent logic and strained exegesis. That which cannot be reconciled remains unreconciled despite clever disguises. Like Humpty Dumpty, all the king's horses and all the king's men cannot put together a biblically acceptable case for Christians to pursue self-love—no matter how it is repackaged.

Because such attempts are continually being made, perhaps it would be profitable to evaluate one such effort. The example I have in mind is not from the writings of a Christian psychologist at all. Rather, it is from the pen of a well-known evangelical theologian and spokesman, John R. W. Stott.

In his important and well-written book, *The Cross of Christ*, Stott discusses his view on Christian self-esteem in a chapter titled, "Self-Understanding and Self-Giving." Stott comes out against self-love in this chapter, which is all to the good, but at the same time stoutly maintains it is necessary for Christians to "affirm" themselves in Christ. He insists that such self-affirmation is an important dimension of the message of the cross. This is not good at all.

The question might be asked, "What is the difference between expressions of self-love and expressions of self-affirmation?" The answer proves to be more semantic than substantive. However, let us first review Dr. Stott's case for self-affirmation and then evaluate it.

Let us pick up Dr. Stott's discussion of Christian self-affirmation with his comment, "The cross revolutionizes our attitude to ourselves as well as to God." This means we can only answer the question of who am I and how am I to view myself with the cross in mind.[1]

Stott prefaces his discussion by strongly maintaining that we live in an era rife with "crippling inferiority feelings" and "low self-esteem." The causes of this widespread and debilitating condition are varied: deprived childhoods, rejection, a ruthless, competitive society, political, economic and racial oppressions, a technological world that converts people into ciphers and behavioral theories that reduce man to a conditioned response. "No wonder," Stott claims, "many people today feel worthless nonentities."[2]

Stott wisely rejects the human potential movement as an answer, rightfully calling it a form of self-worship which teaches the inherent goodness of man, his need to accept himself unconditionally and actualize his potential.[3] Stott also decries the fact that many Christians have allowed "themselves to be sucked into this movement." Even worse, in his estimation, is that these Christians seek to justify doing so on the basis of the Second Great Commandment. Thankfully, Stott has little patience with such a position. "Self-love is a fact to be recognized," he writes, "and a rule to be used, not a virtue to be commended."[4] In other words, self-love is not something man needs to "learn" to do.

But Stott next poses the "Juliet" question. "How then should we regard ourselves so that we are neither loving ourselves unseemly nor hating ourselves unnecessarily?" The answer, he believes, is found in the cross of Christ which "calls us both to self-denial and self-affirmation."[5]

By self-denial, Stott means we are to turn our backs on ourselves, crucifying the old nature and dying to self in a threefold manner. First we die to the very principle of sin itself. Second, we die daily to self. This is "something which we must deliberately do ourselves," he writes, "though by the power of the Spirit, putting our old nature to death." Finally, there must be our death to ease and safety, and a willingness to suffer persecution.[6]

But self-denial is only half the story, according to Stott. There is another theme in Scripture that runs "alongside Jesus' explicit call to self-denial," and this "is His implicit call to self-affirmation," which, Stott maintains, "is not at all the same thing as self-love."[7]

That is an intriguing disclaimer. How does Stott support it? By appealing to Jesus. Stott says that anyone who reads the Gospels would find it next to impossible to believe Jesus "had a negative attitude to human beings Himself, or encouraged one in others." Stott contends that by His teachings, His attitude and His purpose for coming, Jesus proved the opposite was true—He valued others highly.

In His discourses, Jesus spoke of people's created value— that is, that we are made in God's image and likeness. Stott writes approvingly of this self-declaration made by a college student: "I'm me and I'm good, 'cause God don't make junk." That may be poor grammar, Stott observes, "but it was good theology."[8]

Not only did Jesus talk about our value, but by His attitude it is obvious that He "despised nobody and disowned nobody," Stott says. He welcomed the system's outcasts and rejects, ministered to the poor and hungry, and associated with "sinners." Therefore, in many ways, "Jesus acknowledged their value and loved them, and by loving them He further increased their value."[9]

Finally, in His purpose for coming and in His resolve to suffer and die for us, we see how greatly He valued us. "It is only when we look at the cross that we see the true worth of human beings," Stott writes.[10]

Thus, according to Stott, the cross offers proof of the "value of the human self" and at the same time vividly portrays how we are to deny that self. How can we integrate those apparent opposites? Stott believes we can do this by understanding that we are neither wholly good nor wholly bad, but rather a mixture of both. Thus we have both a "true self" and a "false self," which came about as a result of the Adamic fall. The self we deny and disown is our false self, which consists of all those characteristics that are incompatible with the person of Christ. The self we "affirm and value" is the created self, which includes all "within us" that is compatible with Christ.

What are we to affirm about ourselves? Those created characteristics such as our rationality, our sense of moral obligation, our families, our hunger for love and community, our consciousness of God's "transcendent majesty" and our "inbuilt urge" to bow low "and worship Him." Granted, Stott concedes, this part of self has been "twisted" by sin, but nonetheless "Christ came to redeem it." Therefore "we must gratefully and positively affirm it."[11]

Also, along with our created characteristics, Christians are to affirm their "re-created" attributes, their new selves "created to be like God in true righteousness and holiness." The transforming experience we undergo when we become Christians "also changes our self-image," according to Stott. "We now have much more to affirm, not boastfully but gratefully."[12]

Because our self-image in Christ is a positive one, Stott thinks it is wrong for believers to use such words as *worthless* or *worthlessness* when speaking of themselves. Unworthy yes, but worthless, no. If Jesus has declared us valuable, how can we dare say we are worthless? Stott further says that "a vital part of our self-affirmation . . . is what we have become in Christ." We can have a positive sense of self-worth because God has accepted us in Christ.[13]

Stott concludes his discussion of self-affirmation by claiming every believer is part Jekyll and part Hyde. On the one hand we have dignity, nobility, etc., because we are created in God's image; on the other hand, because we are fallen, we also exhibit depraved characteristics. "My true self," Stott writes, "is what I am by creation, which Christ came to redeem, and by calling. My false self is what I am by the Fall, which Christ came to destroy."[14]

Self-denial and self-affirmation—Stott claims that the cross teaches us both are valid responses for the believer. For him, the cross reveals both the "God-given measure" of the self's true worth and the "God-given model for the denial of our false self," which is to be crucified.[15]

## Critiquing the Argument

Well—there we have Dr. Stott's argument. Affirming ourselves to ourselves is good and necessary, and most important, biblical in an age in which people are crushed by feelings of inferiority and see themselves as nothings. Is he right? Does he have a solid scriptural foundation for his reasoning? Or is this an example of bent logic and labored semantics?

Let us begin where Stott begins—the character of our present age. He believes this is an age of "crippling inferiority feelings" and rampant low self-esteem due to the conditions of life around us. Yet if we compare our world with the New Testament world, we might have a difficult time proving that ours is an age especially conducive to creating low self-esteem.

The New Testament world wasn't exactly noted for its uplifting social environment. Degrading slavery, appalling poverty, uncontrolled diseases, abortion and infanticide, abandoned children by the tens of thousands, male and female prostitution, and a demonic world-order that kept people in abject fear and superstition are just a few of the social realities of that period. Was this a place for happy childhoods and adult "actualization"? Yet Scripture does not present a need to encourage New Testament believers to affirm their created value so that they might offset devastating feelings of inferiority.

Stott's claim that the cross calls us to affirm ourselves, or that Jesus "implicitly calls us to self-affirmation," stretches the limits of the text of Scripture and moves us into the realm of eisegesis. Having bought into the self-esteem doctrine by paying dearly in scriptural consistency, Stott must now rationalize the high price.

When one looks at all Scripture clearly says about the cross, it seems strange to hear anyone say the cross calls us to self-affirmation. I can readily say the cross calls me to self-denial (Luke 14:26-33). I could also say that it calls me to repent (Acts 2:22-39), to deny self in humility and servant-hood (Philippians 2:5-8), to suffer, even unjustly if called upon (1 Peter 2:20-25), to die to the world and glory in the cross (Galatians 6:14), and to evaluate the sincerity of my faith (2 Corinthians 13:5). But as I survey the New Testament, I cannot think of any Scripture that tells me the cross calls me to affirm my self-worth to myself and others.

Perhaps that is why Stott's case is so heavily dependent on the word *implied*. He speaks of Jesus' implied calling to self-affirmation—a calling he believes is as real as the one to pick up our cross daily and follow Christ, which, of course, is a very explicit call to die to self (Luke 9:23). Stott grounds his argument on what he identifies as the teachings, attitude and purpose of Christ's incarnation. Let us look closely at them one more time.

## The Significance of the Incarnation

Certainly it is true that in His teachings and attitude Jesus showed great compassion for lost mankind. How could we expect anything less from Him who "came from the Father, full of grace and truth"? As the author of Hebrews wrote:

> Since the children have flesh and blood, he too shared in humanity. . . made like his brothers in every way, in order that he might become a merciful and faithful high priest in service to God, and that he might make atonement for the sins of the people (Hebrews 2:14,17).

The wreck that sin had made of us (and this is the key) deeply touched our Lord while here on earth. How terribly deformed the image had become! In making such statements as "God don't make junk," or "He despised nobody and disowned nobody," or "He acknowledged their value and loved them, and by loving them He further increased their value," Stott overstates his case. He ignores all that Jesus had to say about various groups.

True, Jesus spoke of people having more value than sparrows and sheep, but did He say these things so that people could feel better about themselves?[16] Wasn't He primarily pointing out God's compassionate disposition toward us despite our sinful hearts, rather than providing self-esteem "highs" for a people wracked with feelings of inferiority? I can't help wondering if He wasn't also rebuking us, because in our self-love we often don't treat our neighbor as having more value than our animals (see Luke 13:10-17), and we often don't think God values us as we think we ought to be valued (see Mark 10:26-31). When we study the Gospels, we find that Jesus often spoke harshly. He may not have disowned anyone, but He certainly came close.

In Matthew 11, Jesus curses the cities of Korazen, Bethsaida and Capernaum. It would be better for the city of Sodom on the day of judgment than for these cities, He said.

Was Christ disowning these people because of their hard hearts? How did this cursing increase their personal value? In Luke 11:29, He calls the crowd following Him a "wicked generation." He calls people hypocrites in Luke 12:56, and in John 8:44 He accuses the Jews of being sons of the devil. Which of these remarks are exactly value-enhancing statements?

In Matthew 23, Jesus pronounces seven soul-chilling woes upon the Pharisees and teachers of the law. Then He says this to them: "You snakes! You brood of vipers! How will you escape being condemned to hell?" (Matthew 23:33). Dr. Stott notwithstanding, this is strong medicine. Considering the severity of Christ's condemnation of this group, we can only wonder how His words "further increased their value." Can this be considered disowning someone?

Exactly how did people's value increase because Jesus loved them? In what way? And to whom? If Stott means Jesus made it possible for them to enhance their own personal esteem (and I think this is his intent), then we must ask if Jesus is being interpreted properly. People already loved themselves—sinfully so. Would not increasing an already over-inflated opinion of themselves only entrench them deeper in their self-centeredness? Many of these people whom Jesus loved apparently turned against Him and some even demanded His crucifixion.

Wasn't Jesus' real desire to teach them to value their neighbor as much as they already valued themselves? By His every word and deed, Jesus taught people to be as equally concerned with their neighbors' well-being as with their own and to be as equally willing to put out the resources and time to prove it. I do not think this is what Stott meant, however, when he made his "increased value" statement.

It appears as if Stott may be swallowing camels and straining gnats when he finds a call to self-affirmation in the words and attitude of Jesus. Perhaps it would be closer to the intent of Scripture to say that Jesus sought to reveal by His words and actions the true nature of God to a people completely blinded to it by their sin (Mark 7:6-23). He did this not to increase their sense of personal self-worth, but rather to free them from their slavery to self-idolatry and restore them to a right relationship with their Creator.

How wonderfully this is illustrated with the episode of the blind man at Jericho in Luke 18:35-43. The blind man cried out to Jesus for mercy (vs. 38). Though rebuked by "those who led the way," he did not cease his strident pleas. Only Jesus could do what needed to be done. Then Luke tells us:

> Jesus stopped and ordered the man to be brought to him. When he came near Jesus asked him, "What do you want me to do for you?"
>
> "Lord, I want to see," he replied.
>
> Jesus said to him, "Receive your sight; your faith has healed you."
>
> Immediately he received his sight and followed Jesus, praising God. When all the people saw it, they also praised him.

Let us imitate them.

## Does the Cross Show Our Value?

Stott not only bases his claim for self-affirmation on Jesus' words and attitude, but also on our value as revealed by the cross, that is, our value "by creation, which Christ redeems, and by calling." Since I have already listed some of what he believes to be our created and recreated characteristics that we are to affirm, I will not do so here.

Let it suffice to say that indeed "God don't make junk." But I cannot say I am "good" because man, by his sinful rebellion, made junk out of what God created. As Joseph Alleine wrote:

> O miserable man, what a deformed monster has sin made you! God made you "little lower than the

angels"; sin has made you little better than the devils.[17]

True, God created us with many abilities and talents—to the praise of His glory. He also placed us as His vice-regents over the earth to use these abilities and talents—also to the praise of His glory. Likewise, this service to Him was our glory and greatness, truly reflecting our creation in His image and likeness. These are wonderful and humbling truths. Yet, it is also true that we have taken every one of them and used them against Him—robbing Him of His glory and losing ours.

My sin has left me without any claim on God as His valuable creature and forfeited any right to mercy. The wonder is that He has given me life at all, let alone the richly gifted one I possess in Christ. The truth of the matter is that whatever created value I have will not keep me out of hell if I will not cast myself at Jesus' feet in genuine repentance for my sins.

**Since the Fall, the issue for mankind is not how we were made (in God's image) but what we have become**. The issue is not our value but what we deserve. The issue is not our self-esteem but our depravity. The issue is not what I am worth, but how can I become reconciled with God. My "created value" plays no role in such a confrontation. What matters is whether I am "in Christ." God created me in His image, but He is under no obligation to save me because of that, nor love me as He does. My sinful self is not a false self; it is what I am at birth. We are "by nature objects of wrath" (Ephesians 2:3) and will stay that way unless we are made new creations in Christ.

When we seek to use the created value argument to deliberately bolster someone's self-esteem and claim it is necessary and biblical to do so, because so many are racked with feelings of inferiority, we do a great disservice to the Gospel. We even misuse the argument. We appear to be trying to offset what we think is the terrible picture of sinful man expressed so starkly in Scripture.

Yet this is the picture God has chosen to emphasize. When Ephesians 2:3 or John 3:36 tells us we are under God's wrath, it is difficult to see a better self-esteem based on our created value as one of man's needs. These verses affirm our destiny, not our value. And that destiny is not presented to us from within the gentle confines of our created value.

This is what God wants us to understand—and it is of vital importance that we do so. When speaking of our created value, we should do so only as an apologetic support for the doctrine of depravity, as Alleine did in his words quoted above. Look at what you were meant to be! Now look at what you have become!

The "good news" is not that we have discovered our created value and therefore are at liberty to affirm ourselves. The "good news" is that the wrath of God toward sinful, self-loving, rebellious man has been propitiated by Christ's death on the cross, making a way for men to be reconciled to God.

Those who seek to use the created value argument are basing their premise not on Scripture but on the "discovered" truth of humanistic psychology—a dangerous foundation indeed. For humanistic psychology teaches that man's basic problem is not that he has a sin nature (rooted in self-love) or that he sins naturally and purposely, but rather that he has low self-esteem, stemming from a massive, others-induced inferiority complex, which in turn leads him to make "wrong choices" in his search for love and self-worth.

Under the influence of "Christian" psychology, the emphasis continues to shift from man's sin to his "sickness," from sinful man to pathological man. The obvious cure for such a person is to make him feel better about himself. It is equally obvious that the cross can never supply the needed boost.

What Scripture has to say about man's created value is being taken out of its biblical context and its present subordinate relation to the cross. Instead, it is being used to compete with, and even criticize, a clear and convicting message: that we who are called to follow Christ are called to die to self. By saying that the cross teaches me to affirm my true self-value,

Stott distracts us from what the cross truly affirms—the great love of God ("expressed in his kindness to us in Christ Jesus") over against the depths of my worthless sinfulness.

## Unworthy or Worthless?

Yes, my worthlessness. Stott says I mustn't use that word. He criticized Elizabeth Clephane for using that word in her hymn, "Beneath the Cross of Jesus." What she wrote was this:

> And from my smitten heart with tears,
> Two wonders I confess—
> The wonder of His glorious love,
> And my own worthlessness.

Was she wrong using *worthlessness* the way she did? Was she not simply drawing attention to the fact that she was overcome with wonder that God would save such a worthless sinner as she?

Unworthy, Stott says, but not worthless. Is he right? Has Clephane misunderstood grace and the purpose of the cross? I don't think so.

First, we might seek to understand the difference between the words. Stott takes *unworthy* to mean undeserving. Yet when I open the second edition of Webster's unabridged dictionary, I find the first definition listed for the word *unworthy* reads "without merit or value: worthless." Sweet irony. Basically, the words mean the same thing. So why the fuss? Could it be that those who are intent on affirming themselves prefer words that carry less negative connotations than words such as *worthless*? The latter may come too close to old-fashioned "worm" theology for our modern taste.

It is also fascinating to note that Romans 3:12 in the NIV reads, "All have turned away, they have together become worthless." The KJV reads "unprofitable" and the NASB uses the word *useless*. Here we have God's perspective on man-the-sinner. Whichever word you choose, it isn't terribly value-enhancing. The Greek word translated "worthless" is *achreioo* and conveys the idea of something being worthless, useless, or unprofitable, to the point of replusiveness.

Thus it could be said that sin has made me so worthless in God's sight that He is repulsed by me. Given the surrounding context of Romans 3:12, one can readily accept this interpretation.

Have you ever heard the expression, "The very sight of you makes me sick"? In a sense, this is what God is saying to all those outside of Christ. Psychologists would tell us that we would cause our children serious emotional problems if we spoke to them in such terms. Yet here is God saying that to those who do not have Christ as their Lord and Savior. *Worthless* used in this way is quite a step beyond *unworthy* as used by Stott to mean "undeserving." We can sing Elizabeth Clephane's hymn after all.

Now, it is very true that in Christ God loves me as much as He loves His own dear Son. Who can fathom such love? It doesn't matter. Though I cannot fathom it, I can glory in it! Even more, much more, I bow low in awe before Him over the wonder of it all. That I, a worthless sinner, should become God's precious, adopted son—cleansed and purified and clothed in the robes of Christ's righteousness. Even my faith is His gift. What grace!

Does that grace then invite me to turn the cross of Christ into a personal virtue that enthralls me, or into a liberating truth that allows me to see my real problem as inferiority—rather than carnality—so that I can "cure" it with pleasant murmurings of self-affirmation? The answer should be obvious.

God loves me, yes. Wonders of wonders! I can only begin to appreciate what all this means, and what my response ought to be, with the help of these words from the hymn "Beneath the Cross of Jesus":

> I take, O cross, thy shadow
> For my abiding place

I ask no other sunshine than
The sunshine of His face;
Content to let the world go by,
To know no gain or loss,
My sinful self my only shame,
My glory all the cross.

"Worthy is the lamb, who was slain," wrote the Holy Spirit through His servant John, "to receive power and wealth and wisdom and strength and honor and glory and praise" (Revelation 5:12). We need to stress anew that the cross teaches us the great value of our Savior, not ourselves, that it is He who must be affirmed, not ourselves; that it is He who is to be esteemed by you and me—not you and me esteeming ourselves to ourselves.

I can only say once more that no one can simultaneously face the cross and a mirror. To say that the cross and Christ Himself teach us to both die to self and affirm self is not a paradox but a contradiction. And changing terms does not change a bad teaching.

If being able to verbally affirm myself to myself is so important, why didn't God make it more obvious in the pages of Scripture? Why did He so carefully obscure it that His church had to wait two thousand years for the rise of "Christian" psychology before it could understand the total "implications" of the cross?

I also wonder why the call for self-denial does not include my preoccupation with my self-worth or esteem or love or affirmation. I wonder about a Christianity so insecure and lacking in faith that it must be constantly writing and speaking self-affirming words about itself to itself. I wonder what now drives us to put this so close to the center of our attention.

When all is said and done on this issue, the center of my focus is me. Self-esteem, self-worth, self-love, self-affirmation—no matter which term we use, it is hard to escape the strong lure that attends the word *self*. It is the lure of pride and me-centeredness. Where does Jesus fit in this preoccupation with my esteeming myself to myself? For that which pre-occupies my thoughts, the same receives my devotion.

I do not know about others, but I lack the expertise to trace out the vague line between a "biblical" self-esteem and a "carnal" self esteem. Is there one? The idea that we study Scripture to find support for my "need" for an appropriate sense of self-esteem is foreign to Scripture. I am almost shocked by the aggressiveness of some in pursuing self-esteem and insisting it is biblical.

Why do we have so much trouble understanding that the central focus of the Scriptures is not me or my self-worth, but rather God and His glorious attributes exhibited in Christ Jesus? We were created and redeemed to praise Him.

What exactly is a proper self-esteem, or an appropriate self-love, or a rightly expressed affirmation of myself? How do I recognize it? When do I realize I have achieved it? Who decides these things? How do we know we are being objective or in accord with the Spirit? We can't, of course, because the whole process is so subjective that it defies scriptural control.

The writer of Hebrews reminds us that the animal bodies of the sin offering were taken outside the camp and burned. "Jesus also suffered outside the city gate," he says, "to make the people holy through his blood." Knowing this, we are to "go to him outside the camp, bearing the disgrace he bore. For here we do not have an enduring city, but we are looking for the city to come" (Hebrews 13:12,13).

Let us allow something George Muller said to serve as a compelling explanation of these verses and the final word on our discussion of self-affirmation as defended by Stott.

When asked the reason for his success, Muller did not answer, "I have learned to deny myself as well as esteem myself to myself because of what Christ has done for me." No, what he said was:

> There was a day when I died, utterly died; died to George Muller, his opinions, preferences, tastes and will—died to the world, its approval or censure— died to the approval or blame even of my brethren

and friends—since then I have studied only to show myself approved unto God.[18]

Muller never seemed bogged down over his need for self-affirmation. Nor, for that matter, with loathing himself. His chief concern seemed two-fold: to make the excellent reality of his Lord known to all and to delight himself in his God. He seems to have succeeded remarkably well.

Apparently Muller, as have thousands upon thousands of believers throughout history, simply rejoiced and accepted what Scripture taught: "I consider everything a loss compared to the surpassing greatness of knowing Christ Jesus my Lord, for whose sake I have lost all things. I consider them rubbish, that I may gain Christ . . ." (Philippians 3:8).

---

## Notes

1   John R. Stott. *The Cross of Christ*. Downers Grove: Intervarsity Press, 1986, p. 274.

2   *Ibid.*

3   *Ibid.*, p. 275.

4   *Ibid.*, p. 276.

5   *Ibid.*

6   *Ibid.*, p. 280.

7   *Ibid.*, p. 281.

8   *Ibid.*

9   *Ibid.*

10 *Ibid.*

11 *Ibid.,* pp. 282, 283.

12 *Ibid.,* p. 283.

13 *Ibid.,* p. 284.

14 *Ibid.,* p. 285.

15 *Ibid.*

16     One of the interesting bits of information that has become buried under psychology's avalanche of claims that we all have low self-esteem and thus need to love ourselves more is that the facts don't necessarily support this assertion.

David G. Myers, in his book *The Inflated Self*, draws attention to the fact that:

> Although it is popularly believed that most people suffer from the "I'm not OK—your OK" syndrome, research indicates that William Saroyan was much closer to the truth: "Every man is a good man in a bad world—as he himself knows." (p. 21.)

Myers then offers a number of examples to support his position, including a College Board high school aptitude test question which asked high-schoolers to compare themselves with their peers. According to Myers, "Judging from their responses in the most recent years for which data are available, it appears that America's high school students are not racked with inferiority feelings" (p. 24). Myers then makes the following observation:

> Note how radically at odds this conclusion is with the popular wisdom that most of us suffer from low self-esteem and high disparagement. . . . But most

of us are not groveling about with feelings that everyone else is better than we are (p. 24).

17 *The Golden Treasury of Puritan Quotes*, compiled by I. D. E. Thomas (Chicago: Moody Press, 1975), p. 266.

18 Roger Steer, "Seeking First the Kingdom," *Discipleship Journal*, Issue 35 (1985), p. 24.

# 5

# Into the Wilderness of Victimization

The words we use in everyday conversation reveal a great deal about our world view. More than we realize they reflect the way we interpret reality. It isn't a deliberate thing we do, but nonetheless we make our position known.

For instance, consider the word *feel*. A fine word, an expressive word, a word much misused in our society. Why do people almost invariably say, "I feel such and such is true" when they really mean "I believe (or think) such and such is true"? Feelings do not articulate thoughts.

I recently read a paper in which a student was outlining a famous social thinker's four-point philosophy of education. As the student explained each point, he used these words: "So and so felt. . . ." Now, I'm sure this philosopher of education did have feelings, even about his philosophy, but he had also clearly thought it out and articulated it. This student's choice of words exemplifies a trend in our society, which increasingly favors an emotion-based vocabulary to express life—the legacy, perhaps, of a generation desperate to get in touch with its inner-self.

One of the primary agents responsible for this word shift is psychology. The vocabulary of psychology has become the commonplace means to describe reality. For example, we classify those guilty of the most debased sin, such as child molesting, as "sick" or "diseased." These words convey an entirely different view of man than the word *sinner*.

What has really made me somber is that Christians haven't proved the least bit shy in joining this trend. More and more we hear psychological terms replacing biblical ones—so much so that it is beginning to impact the way we understand Christianity. So much so that one Christian "expert" on codependency said, ". . . the goal of recovery [from codependency] and of Christianity are the same: healthy human behavior that works."[1]

Strange—when did the goal change? All this time I have believed the goal of Christianity was to show in the coming ages "the incomparable riches of his grace, expressed in his kindness to us in Christ Jesus" (Ephesians 2:7).

One phrase in particular shows the enormous influence of psychology on Christians. It is the phrase, "People are hurting," and it reflects a serious alteration in the way we think about and convey the Gospel. This was highlighted for me recently at one of our chapel services. The young spokesman for a visiting singing group exhorted us to "share Jesus with people because they are hurting."

How often we hear that phrase these days! We read it in missionary letters, hear it from the pulpit and run across it in the conversations of a wide variety of believers. A few years back, Christians would have said, "People are lost sinners going to hell. They need to be told about Jesus." Indeed, every great awakening and missions movement has been impelled by this dreadful knowledge. The substitution of "people are lost" with "people are hurting" shows how deep and subtle are the inroads of psychology upon Christian thinking.

I doubt many of us are aware of the substitution. But with the phrase, "People are hurting," has also come a conceptual substitution. The phrase connotes acceptance of the psychological concept of victimization. This is true not only in our understanding of sin, but also in our understanding of sanctification.

With its emphasis on victimization and our feelings of pain, "Christian" psychology has shifted our focus from the cognitive and objective to the purely emotional and subjective. This has brought about a tendency to deal with sin in terms of feelings alone, rather than in terms of underlying motives, thoughts, and the resulting actions as illuminated by Scripture. This tendency is just the opposite of what God did when He confronted Cain. (See Genesis 4:2-7.) God denied that Cain had a right to feel the way he did. Such is not the case today. Let me relate one interesting example of this.

The bishops of the Episcopal Church, after barely defeating a motion that would allow the ordination of practicing homosexuals, passed a motion that read in part:

> We recognize that it would not be faithful to the Gospel to ignore the **anguished cries** of homosexual men and women who **feel hurt, rejected** and **angry** by what they see about them. At the same time, we recognize it would not be faithful to the Gospel to ignore or simply label as homophobic the **anguished cries** of men and women who **feel hurt, rejected** and **angry** that what they see as sin is not being reaffirmed as such.[2] (Emphasis added.)

What! Is no one concerned with scriptural truth here?!

Emotional self-awareness of our victimization has become the new and favored pathway to Christian maturity. As we will see, not only are the unsaved victims, but the saved are also victims learning to overcome their victimization. It would not be out of line to call them "recovering victims."

## Sanctification thru Victimization Therapy?

Now, this is a strange pathway to maturity, and not one easily discernible in Scripture. The fact that so many believers—pastors, teachers, counselors, housewives, businessmen and what have you—have embraced it with uncritical enthusiasm shows just how deeply the evangelical community has accepted the pathological view of man.

While I cannot give a definitive answer as to why this is so, I will show that it is radically at odds with the Word of God. I will show that there is no way it can be integrated with a consistent, scriptural world view or with the biblical doctrine of progressive sanctification. In fact, a pathological world view threatens to destroy these teachings. We cannot integrate world views that fundamentally contradict one another. At least one of them must be altered in the process.

Perhaps the best way to dramatize these differences is to combine a little imagination with a great deal of fact. This chapter will provide the imagination. Let us take a step into the distant past, visit with the apostle Paul, and listen in on an imaginary conversation. Then in the next chapter we will take a closer look at the issues we raise here.

\* \* \*

Paul is sitting at a table in his rented house in Rome. The year is A.D. 61. On the table in front of him are two or three opened parchment scrolls. Off in one corner lounges a Roman soldier, reminding us that Paul is under house arrest and is awaiting his trial or, more likely, his soon release. The case against him is very weak.

The apostle has not let his circumstances keep him from preaching the Gospel to anyone with ears, great or small, friend or foe. Nor have they prevented him from carrying on a vigorous correspondence with the churches in Macedonia and the province of Asia—exhorting, correcting and teaching them sound doctrine. At this moment, sitting at the table with Paul, is his amanuensis with his quill pen scratching furiously as Paul speaks. Paul is writing to the young church at Colosse, and even as he dictates we instantly recognize the "verses"—Colossians 3:1-17. As Paul concludes verse seventeen, he turns to two other men whom we haven't noticed until now.

Surprisingly, these men are dressed in latter 20th century business suits and have a certain air about them that allows us to make an immediate identification. Yes, these are Christian psychologists! They sit there, looking slightly uncomfortable on their first-century chairs. One of them, short, stocky and bearded, is nervously crossing and recrossing his ankles. Periodically he pushes his glasses up on his nose or peers seriously over the heavy plastic rims. The other gentleman is sitting immobile, his rounded shoulders relaxed and his head tilted slightly forward. In his left hand he is flicking the button on a ball point pen, which causes a metallic clicking sound to fill the room.

The noise brings an irritated glance from the amanuensis as he finishes writing and dips his reed pen into the inkpot by his right hand.

"You see, gentlemen," Paul begins. "Someone is trying to undermine the confidence of our Colosse brethren in the sufficiency of our Lord Jesus Christ. Oh, how I wish I could go there personally to confront the scoundrels! This letter must do for the moment. If they will but focus on our risen Lord and mortify the flesh by the power of the Holy Spirit, I know they will emerge victorious. Ah, but they must see that Christ and Christ alone is their sufficiency! They need no other mediators. Only in this way will they be able to become like Him within their hearts and in their actions. There is nothing like the reality of Christ's power to strengthen a believer's faith. What do you think, good sirs? Shall I add more? Do you have a word of encouragement to send?"

There is a pause as the two psychologists glance at one another. Then the one playing with his ball point pen answers. The name tag attached to the lapel of his suit coat reads "Secundus."

"Well, as far as it goes, Paul, it is excellent. Christians need to know that wrong behavior is unacceptable. However, I am not sure you are touching the deep hurts of their hearts with those words." Secundus pauses, looking intently at the floor as if expecting to find the proper words inscribed there.

A dull clicking spills into the silence. He hasn't noticed Paul's eyebrows arching quizzically.

At this point the other psychologist breaks in. His name tag reads "Guessius." Peering over the top of his glasses, he says, "Yes, Paul, you must realize most people are really responding in ways that reflect the nature of their victimization."

"Pardon me?" Paul answers.

"Well, you see, Paul," Guessius continues, "people are filled with denied pain, they are hurting from the numerous disappointments they have received living in a world that cannot love them the way they longed to be loved."

"Ah, perhaps now I understand the gist of what you are saying," Paul interrupts. "Yes, yes, sin has wrecked us all and the consequences have been tragic. By nature we have all become objects of wrath. We have all turned away, and together have become worthless."

"Uh, ah—*unworthy* would be a better word, Paul. After all, if Christ died for us, it seems wrong to call ourselves worthless." Secundus is speaking again, nervously. (Click, click goes his pen.) "But I think you have missed Guessius' point. We must see ourselves as victims if we are to understand our culpability as sinners." (Again Paul's brow furrows.) "And we must take this into serious consideration when we are exhorting believers to imitate Christ. I like the way one of my colleagues has expressed it. He said that 'before we'll see how sinful we are as a self-protective agent, we must first feel how disappointed we are as vulnerable victims.' "

"Yes, Paul," Guessius injects, "all of us have been victimized to one extent or another. Some people have been cruelly and brutally abused and they have zero self-esteem. These hidden hurts drive them to seek love and esteem in destructive and even addictive patterns that lock them into a life of despair and defeat. Even Christians are trapped by these things and no matter how much they pray or read Scripture or try to obey God, they can't break free."

"Wait just a moment, please!" Paul responds, his voice edged with sharpness. "I cannot accept the direction your words are leading. Truly, we suffer the consequences of our slavery to sin and receive many painful wounds in the process. But two things need to be kept uppermost in our minds. First, all of us have sinned and fall short of the glory of God—no small matter to a holy God! We are by nature sinners and deserve His wrath. I do not think I have heard you two mention this basic fact. We cannot downplay this with talk of disappointments and low self-esteem. God calls sinners to the cross. Christ came into the world to save sinners. Outside Christ men live in malice and envy, hating and being hated—so yes, people do hurt one another. I did. I destroyed many. But God is rich in mercy.

"Second, and most important, remember that in Christ all are new creations. The old has passed and the new has come. Sin no longer has dominion over us. The old man was crucified with Christ. Whatever happened before I came to Christ no longer matters. God is now for me, not against me. The same power that raised Christ from the dead works on my behalf also."

"Well, what you are saying isn't exactly the whole picture," Secundus hesitantly answers (click, click). "You see, Paul, even when people accept Christ they can still be caught up in compulsive and unacceptable behavior. They can't help themselves. It is as if something inside them voicelessly tells them, 'This is the way to find meaning and love,' or 'This is the way to compensate for the rejection you suffered while growing up.' The bad conditioning they received as children put an unconscious barrier between them and God's grace. More than just exhortations to think on Jesus above are needed. Such people require extensive professional help, years of counseling perhaps, before they can work free of their bondage."

"Secundus," Paul answers, "do you understand what you are saying? The one outside Christ is truly in great bondage. But to his own lusts, not because of some past victimization. It is in his heart to do so. As for those who are in Christ, well,

do you not know that God has promised to meet the needs of
His people with the riches that are ours in Christ Jesus? He
has promised that none of us are tempted beyond what we
can bear. Do you not believe Him? We must not forget that
God's power working in us is able to do far more than we can
think or imagine. Perhaps that 'voiceless something' encouraging one to sin is not bad conditioning, but Satan's whisper-
ings."

"Paul, you mustn't go to such idealistic extremes," Guessius protests. "Just saying 'no' as you are telling the Colossians to do isn't enough. For many, the hurts from the past
are too overwhelming. They drive these people to failure and
despair in their walk with the Lord. It isn't even enough to
tell them to focus on Christ. The damage is too subtle and
enslaving to so easily leave behind. They need someone with
proper training, as Secundus mentioned, to help guide them
back to uncover and emotionally work through these deep
wounds. Only then can they be freed from them—forgiving
and being forgiven. Surely you, of all people, can understand
this?" Guessius emphatically pushes his glasses back on his
nose as he finishes speaking.

"Guessius, why do you empty the cross of Christ of its
power?" Paul answers. "Is He not God's wisdom for us, that
is, our righteousness, holiness and redemption?" (Anger flick-
ers in Guessius' eyes, but Paul continues, his voice now with
a harder edge.) "Let me explain what the Lord has given me,
gentlemen. I live daily with a Satanic messenger that tor-
ments me—and it is the Lord who has done this." (At this
pronouncement, the two psychologists exchange a furtive
glance and Guessius cocks his left eyebrow.)

"So if we want to speak of hurts, well, I can join you, and
mine is from God directly. It is anything but gentle. A
strange thing for a God of 'unconditional love' to do—right?
No. God knows my need and how to meet it. I bow down in
thanksgiving before Him, because through this He has made
known to me His greatness and grace. I could have experienced them in no other way.

"He has told me and taught me that His grace is sufficient to overcome every obstacle that would rob me of my joy
in Him. And His power is magnified and made effective when
I am most helpless. So enough of this talk about how our
painful disappointments keep us from experiencing the obedience of joyful faith! Let us count hardship as discipline from
the Lord, that we might share in His holiness.

"Next, I will say to you what I said to my brothers here in
Rome. Shall we go on sinning so that grace may increase all
the more? God forbid that we should find any excuse to justify doing so. We died to sin when we died with Christ and
have now been raised to new life in Him. Has that no affect
on our so-called painful disappointments? We live this way by
the power of God's grace through faith in Christ. When I compare this with what you are saying, I am reminded of something I wrote to the Galatians. 'Are you so foolish,' I asked
them, 'that having begun with the Spirit, you are now trying
to attain your goal by human effort?'

"Now, Satan will do what he can to have us disbelieve all
of this. He wants us to believe we are still under his control.
And yes, we will have great struggles with the flesh. I have
experienced them intensely. The flesh wants to go contrary to
everything the Spirit desires of me. Nothing good lives in me,
that is, in my flesh. But thanks be to God—through Jesus
Christ our Lord, I am under no obligation to the flesh.

"God's Spirit lives in me. And the indwelling Spirit is living evidence that God loves me. All this assures me that I can
defeat the demands of the sinful nature. I can obey God and
live a life of righteousness, peace and joy in the Holy Spirit.
No, I am far from perfect. Nonetheless, I press on, thanking
God that nothing can ever again separate me from His love.
But though I am not perfect, I am to be perfecting—perfecting holiness out of a holy fear of God. I have an insatiable
hunger to know Christ. Increasingly this hunger marks my
life and ought to mark the life of every believer."

"You seem almost harsh, Paul," Secundus says. "Let me
present you with a hypothetical situation. You have just told
the Colossians to put to death sexual immorality. Well, sup-

pose one of them can't. In shame and anguish he continually gives way to this sin. This man needs help, not rejection. Bringing his behavior under control isn't sufficient. He must be helped to uncover whatever is unconsciously compelling him to overrule God's command, whatever controls him, whatever tells him that in sexual activity he will find fulfillment. Something in his past has left his sense of self-worth floundering—probably his father failed to affirm him, and he is seeking to affirm himself by his actions—wrongly, I agree. He, too, wishes he could stop but he finds he can't, and it is doubtful he knows why. I say it is wrong to condemn this person. He is a victim caught in the web of his victimization. Can't you see that? Won't you have compassion on such a person?"

"I am willing to be compassionate to any man who is sorrowful over his sin with the godly sorrow God intends. Godly sorrow brings repentance that leads to salvation and leaves no regrets. And salvation, Secundus, means he now has the power to stop his immorality and rejoice in his standing in Christ. Salvation means there is an earnestness and eagerness on his part to show himself approved of God. Of course, there is a worldly sorrow that never touches the heart and leads to death. Tell me, which does your hypothetical fornicator express?

"I think this conversation must come to a close," Paul says, his voice carrying a warning note. "You are saying things that contradict the very words of God. Beware! See to it that no one takes you captive through hollow and deceptive philosophy, which depends on human tradition and the basic principles of this world rather than on Christ. Is not the cross the power of God for the salvation of all who believe? Does God lie when He tells us we can escape temptation?

"Your fornicator is not a victim of anything. He is a self-idolater who worships his own god of lust. It is as Hosea said of Israel, 'Ephraim is joined to idols, leave him alone.' Your sexually immoral man needs to be warned in similar terms. His very actions may indicate he has no part in the kingdom of God. To say he is helpless to change denies God's sovereign power. Why are you offering him excuses by which he can hide from his idolatry? Bring him back to the cross from whence he has wandered, not to his past which has no importance in Christ. At the cross he will find forgiveness. There he will be cleansed; there God's love can be truly experienced; there he will find the power for victory.

"I say again, God calls only the unrighteous to the cross. There they are given a new life in Christ. As I wrote to the Philippians, I have not yet reached perfection, but I press on to take hold of that for which Christ Jesus took hold of me. One thing I do: forgetting what is behind and straining toward what lies ahead, I press on toward the goal to win the prize for which God has called me heavenward in Christ Jesus."

"But that is our point, Paul," Guessius interjects. "It would be wonderful if everyone could do this—but not everyone can because of the way their past has conditioned them. Their past will continue to haunt them until they receive the help they need. All truth is God's truth, Paul, whether revealed or discovered. What we have shared with you is as true as your own words. Your insensitivity will only increase these Christians' sense of rejection, anguish, and hurt and further injure their low self-worth."

"God would not command us to do what is impossible, Guessius," Paul answers, "nor does He lie. Be careful you do not criticize the Holy Spirit! Now I must ask you to go, for I have heard more than I care to. The next thing I know, you will be telling me I was wrong in expelling that wicked, incestuous young man from the Corinthian church for fornicating with his step-mother. Or perhaps you will be second guessing my instructions to the Corinthian brethren not even to eat with those who call themselves Christians but continue in sexual immorality."

Secundus clears his throat nervously. The muffled clicking increases. He looks over at Guessius, who is suddenly preoccupied with cleaning his glasses. "Well, Paul," Secundus begins, inspecting the ceiling, "we have been meaning to speak to you about that . . . ."

## Notes

1   Jim and Phyllis Alsdurf, "The 'Generic Disease,' " *Christianity Today* (December 9, 1988), p. 34.

2   "Bishops Narrowly Reject Homosexual Ordination," *Christianity Today* (October 22, 1990), p. 55.

# 6

# More on
# Victimization

I hope the flight of imagination presented in the last chapter served to set the stage for the discussion that follows. For while the setting was imaginary, the issues are not.

A young woman recently told a mutual friend why she decided to become a psychologist. Psychology, she said, deals with the deep hurts of the heart, whereas Scripture does not. I doubt she came to that position by studying the Bible.

Then why is she of this opinion? A close look at "Christian" psychology's method of counseling, which I have come to call "victimization therapy," may give an answer. It is a methodology that rests on a set of presuppositions that are unbiblical and that raise profound questions concerning the means by which the believer progresses in holiness.

## Self-Esteem and Victimization

Self-esteem and victimization—you can't have one without the other. They are inseparably intertwined. My sense of self-worth is said to depend much on the way I was treated while growing up, especially by my immediate family.

Invariably, according to psychology, my parents failed and my self-esteem suffers because of this. I don't go around saying this to myself, of course, unless maybe I get hold of a book that majors on this theme (of which there is an ample supply). Nonetheless, it is there affecting the way I function relationally with both God and man. If I ever hope to live my Christian life the way God intends, I supposedly must deal with these childhood hurts and disappointments. I must dig them up and relive them emotionally.

The purpose, I am informed, is not to feel sorry for myself or shift blame, but to understand how past hurts and disappointments have held me in bondage, and how they cause me to make "wrong choices." With this information I can free myself from bondage and begin to live a healthy, wholesome Christian life. A noble ambition, but one that seldom comes off as intended through this procedure that finds no support in Scripture.

Dr. Larry Crabb, author of the best-selling book *Inside Out*, probably represents "Christian" psychology as well as anyone in this area. It was his statement on victimization I quoted in our imaginary conversation with Paul. Let me repeat it in our present context. I do so not to single him out, but because his statement concerning victimization strikingly captures a standard article of faith among Christian psychologists.

He claims, "Before we'll see how sinful we are as a self-protective agent, we must first feel how disappointed we are as a vulnerable victim."[1] What does he mean? Basically this: although we have made and continue to make wrong choices, we can never truly understand why or stop repeating them unless we see them in the context of how people have sinned against us when we were dependent upon them and trusted them.

For all practical purposes, this means everyone. Psychology is never shy about numbers and needs. One book on children of alcoholics claims there are twenty-eight million of them, all of whom need "help" to overcome the emotional damage inflicted upon them. If they do not receive this help, then emotionally they will remain children all their lives and will pass on their problems to their children. That is a lot of victims . . . but not a sinner in sight. And we have just begun our list.

Jan Frank, in her book *A Door of Hope*, referring to reports in *Life* magazine and the *Los Angeles Times*, says that "statistics indicate that thirty-four million women in the United states are victims of child sexual abuse." Two sentences later, she writes, "A recent *Los Angeles Times* poll showed that nearly one out of every four people in the United States has been molested. . . ."[2]

That raises the number from 34 million women to 62 million women and men. When we discuss codependency we will see even larger numbers used. One can't help wondering whether there is not a self-serving, self-justifying aspect to using such large numbers.

It seems to make little difference whether one is a believer. According to the view of many Christian psychologists, everyone needs and will benefit from victimization therapy. It should be apparent that this makes a monumental statement concerning the new man in Christ.

The victimization therapy model contains two critical premises. One is the not-so-subtle implication that unless we participate in the process, we will be, at best, only superficial Christians and, at worst, utterly defeated Christians. The second premise is that traditional Christian practices, which are supposed to help us progress in our sanctification, probably can't. So though you may think you are maturing in Christ through such things as Bible study, caring fellowship, and fervent prayer, more than likely it is all an edifice of clay built upon a foundation of denial. This is so because you have not experienced the necessary purging that can only come through victimization therapy.

## How Are We To Deal With Sin?

Victimization therapy dramatically alters the way we view sin and how we are to deal with it. How is the church to counsel a believer in sin, particularly one with habitually sinful behavior? For centuries the church has sought its answers in the Scriptures. Galatians 5 would be a good example of this. There the Word speaks vividly of the Christian's struggle with the flesh and the necessity of those who belong to Christ Jesus to crucify "the sinful nature with its passions and desires" and walk, instead, "in step with the Spirit" (Galatians 5:24,25).

Many New Testament passages give similar counsel. All of them teach that Christ, and Christ only, is to be our glory and our victory. The transforming power of God's love, ministered at the cross, and the reality and sufficiency of our Savior's grace have been understood and believed to be efficacious for all who trusted in Him.

This has all changed under "Christian" psychology. Recently I read an account of how two Christian psychologists had "cured" Christian "sex addicts." One of the "addicts" treated was a practicing homosexual and had been for twenty years.[3] The counselor "discovered" that the root cause of his homosexual behavior was childhood rejection by his family, especially by his father, whose failure to affirm him made him feel unloved, unlovable and no good. Thus he grew up lacking a proper self-worth and developed a deficient personality. As he grew up, other people reinforced this pattern of rejection and low self-esteem.

Even after he married, he still didn't feel loved and cared for until he had his first homosexual experience while attending a Christian college. From that point on he became more and more confirmed in his homosexual behavior. Attempts at reform or counseling from other Christians were failures. He became cynical and bitter toward God, the Bible, and Christianity.

All of this came out through extensive victimization counseling. The pathway to his "cure" was threefold. First a reconciliation with his aged father was brought about. Next, the counselors noticed that whenever he felt rejected (which seemed quite often) their client would seek sex with a male partner. Resisting temptation, then, was not in resisting deviate lust, but rather in resisting his feelings of rejection that in turn fueled feelings of low self-esteem. Homosexual activity would follow to escape these feelings. The counselors helped him "renew his mind and emotions around the issue of rejection." Had this not taken place, they believe, he "could not have repented of sexual sin from the heart."

Third, the psychologists helped him destroy his irrational belief system that held a "negative view of God the Father." This negative view of God—that He would not meet his needs—came about because he "projected the failures of his earthly father onto the heavenly Father." The psychologists accomplished this change by repeatedly washing his "mind with the truth of the Scriptures" in order to "overcome the lies" embedded there. In essence, they reprogrammed him.

The counselors handled another case, briefly mentioned in this article, in the same fashion with the same results. This was about a man who regularly committed adultery with prostitutes, even though he supposedly had a fine relationship with his wife. Victimization counseling uncovered feelings of rejection. At an early age, this man had felt rejected by his father because he was not athletically inclined. This had supposedly caused him to have "serious difficulty believing he was a real man." That, in turn, drove him to seek continual sexual encounters with prostitutes in hopes he would finally have a sexual experience that would give him a sense of real manhood. Of course he never did, so he never stopped trying until "cured" through victimization therapy.[4]

Both of those men continued in their church activities through months and months of counseling. The homosexual's wife is also undergoing counseling for "codependency." She is supposedly addicted to "strength," which developed because "she was the eldest child in an alcoholic family" and thus "became an expert at being codependent." She, we are informed, is harder to "cure" than her homosexual husband.[5]

Does any of this strike you as odd? It does me. I sense a sinking feeling in the pit of my stomach. I simply cannot discern biblical Christianity at work here. Where is the cross, the new man in Christ, the evidence of the indwelling Holy Spirit, the reality of the Son, the pursuit of holiness, the hungering after righteousness, the Godly sorrow before the cross, the warnings of His wrath, the true working of His grace?

Galatians 5:16 warns us not to "gratify the desires of the sinful nature" (or flesh). If we do, we may begin practicing sexual immorality, impurity and debauchery (Galatians 5:19). We are warned in no uncertain terms "that those who live like this will not inherit the kingdom of God" (Galatians 5:21). Read these verses again, because they reasonably explain the behavior of those men. A generation ago, verses like these would have quickly come to mind and, more than likely, been used in counseling—minus any victimization therapy. I do not see how this can be done anymore. To do so would seem unchristian. Why? Because those men and all others like them are now considered to be victims of unwanted lusts, reluctant participants at best.

Perhaps we can find an analogy in the terrorist's hostage, who being brainwashed, becomes a willing compatriot. Alas, these men have been victimized by their parents, robbed of their self-esteem and thus forced into sexual impurity because it was the only way by which they might find self-worth and acceptance. Everything and everyone else had failed them in this regard—even God.

Certainly it would be unkind to accuse them of having willfully "given themselves over to sensuality so as to indulge in every kind of impurity, with a continual lust for more." Who can hold such people accountable to a literal application of the Word of God? It simply doesn't apply to victims. (That, of course, raises this question: To whom then can Scripture be applied, for in psychology we are all victims?)

## Something is Wrong Here

No matter which way we hold it, there is something amiss here. Serious questions are brought to the fore by the theories and methodologies of "Christian" psychology. If the victimization concept is right, then how can we not reject the approach advocated by Scripture?

How, for example, can we defend Peter's harsh treatment of Simon the Sorcerer? (See Acts 8:9-24.) If we look through the lens of "Christian" psychology, we can see that Simon had some serious emotional problems. This is clear from his need to be seen as important by others; it was essential for his sense of self-worth. Probably his father failed to affirm him and his mother had overprotected and dominated him. Yet Peter just runs rough-shod over him.

Peter offers no victimization counseling, no opportunity to feel again those childhood experiences that destroyed his self-esteem. Peter publicly tells Simon he is full of bitterness and captive to sin.

These are not the marks of one who is in Christ. Peter calls on Simon to repent of his wickedness because his heart was not right before God.

Oh, Peter! How could you? Your public condemnation and rejection of Simon will only lower his self-esteem, and his addictive pattern will be reinforced. How could Simon ever see God as a loving God after this, or be able to trust Him again? How could Simon ever repent without first understanding the implications of his own victimization?

Should the reader think I am overstating my scenario let me relate the essence of a sermon delivered by a visiting pastor of counseling from a large and successful evangelical church in southern California. He spoke on the life of Isaac, and the main thrust of his message was that Isaac was a victim all of his life after the traumatic experience of being almost killed by his father. Abraham had violated Isaac's trust in him. He had tricked Isaac into being the sacrifice. Therefore Isaac never trusted Abraham again—nor God for that matter, because God had told Abraham to kill Isaac. And since he didn't trust God, he went against God's prophecy concerning his two sons.

According to this pastor/psychologist, Isaac's life was filled with a pervasive pain that he never worked through. He explained, "Isaac never dealt with the pain in his life. He just buried it and went on. Why else would a man so chosen by God and selected by the Lord deliberately disobey his heavenly Father? He had no idea what was going on inside of his life; he had no idea of the pain in his life. He had no feelings at all. He had no internal validation program. He had just decided that he would never let anyone get close to him in his life again."

How is it possible for this pastor/psychologist to know all that? The obvious point of his sermon was that Isaac was a victim who needed to work through his victimization, but he didn't know how and there was no one to help him. And because he couldn't work it through, he couldn't help disobeying God. However, if we accept this version of the Isaac story, we are faced with a number of difficulties.

First, we must ask ourselves if the reading of Genesis 22:1-19 and 24:61-28:9 supports such a victimization rendering. Did he refuse to let anyone get close to him after he was nearly sacrificed? Did he never trust God again? In Genesis 24:66 we are told Isaac loved Rebekah and that she comforted him after his mother's death. So it appeared he was close to at least these two women. We also know from Genesis 25:28 that Isaac loved Esau.

It is also difficult to say that Isaac never trusted God again. Genesis 26:22-25 seems to indicate a close relation of trust with God. Are we really to believe that God was never able to comfort Isaac, nor win his trust again (if he had ever lost it)? Is God really so inept or Isaac so dense and bitter? What nonsense!

In the New Testament, Isaac is included in the great faith chapter in Hebrews. We must also ask what happens to the analogy of Isaac being an Old Testament picture of Christ if he was tricked, used and victimized by Abraham and God?

Why did Isaac attempt to bless Esau first? I don't know. The text doesn't say, except that Esau was the eldest son. Therefore I am not at liberty to say it was because of Isaac's unresolved pain of victimization that forced him to disobey God. We must read much back into the text before we can extract such a conclusion. The whole sermon bordered on a disrespect for the text of Scripture. It was a blatant attempt to justify victimization therapy as the only rightful means for a believer's sanctification.

If only the church through the ages had understood what we now understand! How much more effective and appealing it could have been! The message of "Christian" psychology is clear: we have taken Scripture too literally and because of this the church has been thoughtless and ignorant as to the complex ways in which sin can imprison us. In the words of Richard Mouw, an ethicist and supporter of "Christian" psychology, "what may start as a simple decision can be difficult to undo. It may take a lot of work. It may take people helping us in complicated and professional ways to undo the power of sin in our lives."[6]

Mouw is not hesitant to claim evangelicals have been less than sensitive "to the ways in which one person's bondage can be passed on to another person" without the recipient being able to reject it. For example, Mouw points out, babies can be born addicted to heroin because their mothers are addicted. And so it is with other forms of bondage, Mouw believes. He says:

> There is a more complicated way in which tendencies to certain addictions—including certain sexual misbehaviors—seems to run in families. I'm convinced there is a genetic propensity to alcoholism. That makes us nervous, because we want to say that if a person is drinking too much, it is her fault; or if a person habitually commits adultery, that's because of a decision he made.[7]

A fascinating remark with profound implications for the authority of Scripture! But before we address the implications, let us address professor Mouw's logic. Is it permissible to compare the physically inherited drug addiction of a newborn with a grown man's lustful propensity to commit adultery? Is Mouw claiming there is no difference? Has he any scientific evidence to support such a comparison? Would he be willing to come forward with scriptural support of such a position?

Professor Mouw also believes some people are genetically preconditioned to become alcoholics.[8] Then are we to believe that adulterers also have some genetic predisposition to adultery? That would be a novel approach to sin.[9] Mouw's unusual logic is characteristic of "Christian" psychology.[10]

There is a much more controversial implication found in Dr. Mouw's statement about the need for professional help, however. He intended to support the claim that Christians can be sinfully addictive (due to victimization) and incapable of breaking free without "people helping us in complicated and professional ways to undo the power of sin in our lives." If this is true, we are left with the disturbing revelation that Scripture must be wrong. There is no way we can come to any other conclusion.

If we are going to say that being in Christ makes no difference in subduing sin; if one must really await the professional attention of a Christian psychologist to take one through victimization therapy before one can be truly free; if the message of the cross has so little power; then I must tearfully conclude that Christianity is a hoax perpetrated upon a race enslaved to sin. For Scripture promises us that "through Christ Jesus the law of the spirit of life set me free from the law of sin and death" (Romans 8:2).

## Victimization on the Mission Field

Let me give one more illustration to dramatize how much the concept of victimization is changing our biblical understanding of sin and salvation and sanctification. I recently received a newsletter from an inner-city mission agency. On the front page was the testimony of a young man who had turned from a life of active homosexuality to a life embracing Jesus.

At the age of 12, J— ran away. But he soon returned home and lived there until the age of 14. At that time his father kicked him out and wouldn't let him return. He lived with various friends for a couple of years and then moved to Florida. There he started his own homosexual prostitution escort service. During this period he also acquired a gay lover with whom he engaged in sadomasochistic behavior.

When J— turned twenty, he attempted to see his family again. His father had him arrested. J— then spent the next sixty days in jail. After his release, the newsletter relates:

> He felt alone and totally rejected by his family. As a result of all this, he views himself as "unlovable" and expects others to enjoy hurting him. How God's heart was breaking as he watched this child being so abused.[11]

J— then moved to California where he immediately became involved with another gay lover. He became more and more depressed and finally called the suicide hotline. The hotline referred him to the inner-city mission. After two weeks under their care, he "gave his life to Jesus." At that point, the mission committed itself to being a friend "who would never reject him," come what may.

Then the mission set about discipling J— and preparing him to get a job, as well as encouraging him to finish his education. But the newsletter cautioned that J— was very fearful of rejection and failure and that he struggled with sticking with the program because he didn't want to face his fears and hurts.

What do you think of that story? Let me say I lift my praise to God if J— has truly repented of his sins and been born again into a new life in Christ Jesus. But that is the very issue about which I have no peace. Perhaps it is the constant emphasis on J—'s "victimization" that keeps me from putting my fears to rest.

Where is the cross in his story? Where is the wicked man who comes to the cross trusting God to justify him through the finished work of Christ on his behalf? Where is the sinner crushed by his sinfulness? Where is the rejoicing sinner praising God for His "amazing grace"? Where is the hunger for the Word, the zest for righteousness, the confidence in Christ, the evidence of the Holy Spirit?

Is it wrong to expect something more than that J— must begin facing and working through his hurts? Could not we hope for something more than the knowledge that J— must work through his feelings of rejection?

Shall I compare J— with the tax-collector in Luke 18:10 or with Tokichi Ichii? Would that be unfair? No matter how many times I read this story, I am forced to wonder whether J— is a sinner at all. The word is never mentioned in the whole testimony. Who can hold him culpable in the face of the declaration that "God's heart was breaking as He watched this child being so abused?"

Again, I have a sinking feeling in my stomach. Is this the Gospel? Something doesn't ring true here. Had his testimony read, "God's heart longs for J— to turn from his wicked life and be reconciled to him through Christ's blood," I could have gladly agreed. But what was said obscures the true condition of J— outside of Christ. We must ask those who wrote his story why they choose to forget that J— is a sinner.

## Pain vs. Sin

Oswald Chambers once wrote that people want religion to be amiable. Would it be out of line to reword this to read, "People want a religion that will not make them feel *painfully* uncomfortable with their sinfulness"? Dr. Chambers also believed, "Every doctrine that is not embedded in the Cross of Jesus will lead astray." He wrote powerfully concerning this:

> . . . very few of us have any understanding of the reason why Jesus Christ died. If sympathy is all that human beings need, then the Cross of Christ is a farce, there was no need for it. What the world needs is not "a little bit of love," but a surgical operation.[12]

Sinners don't need to hear such words as, "Oh you poor thing!" No, what they need to hear is, "Flee God's coming wrath! Flee, sinner, to Jesus Christ on the cross."

By viewing people as victims first, "Christian" psychology seriously inhibits our willingness to believe that the cross has the power to change a sinner. Thus it inhibits our willingness to call sinners to the cross as sinners under God's condemnation. Perhaps the reasoning goes something like this: "Oh, he has been terribly abused. This is not the time to press upon him his sinfulness and warn him of God's wrath. It might crush him and turn him away. He needs to feel the love of God. He needs to feel he is not rejected." But if we do not tell him now, as he stands before the cross, when do we tell him?

Once he "gives his life to Christ," we say, "Ah, he is working through his fears and rejections, his hurts and disappointments. This is no time to press upon him the Lordship of Christ, the demands of discipleship, the picking up of his cross, the authority of Scripture."

But if not now, when? Are we not to make clear the high cost of following Jesus? (See Luke 14:25-35 and Galatians 6:14.)

Things have gotten out of hand. We are uneasy with what the Bible tells us about sinners and salvation and sanctification. Maybe that is why quasi-medical terminology has become so popular. People *hurt*. They have *diseases*. They are *traumatized*. They are *addicted*. They are *dysfunctional*. These words fit into a victimized world much better than the word *sinner* or *rebel* or *wicked*. They carry no sting of culpability. More and more we are substituting them for the word *sin* when we preach the Gospel.

"Christian" psychology is writing a different gospel, one I could almost believe were it not for the old, old story. I could almost be persuaded, were it not for the Scriptures. The Bible faces me in another direction. It turns me toward the cross and says, "Stand here or be lost!"

## Notes

1    Larry Crabb, *Inside Out* (Colorado Springs: NavPress, 1988), p. 185.

2    Jan Frank, *A Door of Hope* (San Bernardino, CA: Here's Life Publishers, 1987), p. 16.

3    Hal B. Schell and Gary Sweden with Betty Reid, "Freeing The Sexually Addicted," *Leadership*, Fall Quarterly (1989), pp. 54-60.

4    *Ibid.*, p. 60.

5    *Ibid.*

6    David Neff, "The Life of Bondage in the Light of Grace: An Interview with Richard Mouw," *Christianity Today* (December 9, 1988), p. 41.
     But it isn't just "neo-evangelicals" who have adopted this view of the necessity of "professionalism" in overcoming sinful "addiction." It has made itself at home in every wing of the evangelical church. Consider this statement by Dr. Gregg R. Albers, Director of Health services at Liberty University:

> Purging oneself from an addictive, stimulating habit is always a difficult, long-term process. Serious addictions require the professional help of a psychiatrist, a mental health professional, or family physician. (Gregg R. Albers, "Sexual Addiction and Believers," *Fundamentalist Journal*, November 1988, p. 35.)

What I found surprising is that no mention is made of the need for a pastor mature in the Word and experience.

7    Neff, *op. cit.*, pp. 41, 42.

8         For years I carried on a ministry to alcoholics at two Los Angeles County rehabilitation centers and became greatly disillusioned with the whole concept of alcoholism as a disease, as well as with the whole apparatus supporting it—including the 12-step method. Now one of the nation's leading experts on alcoholism has taken a similar stance and has raised a veritable hornet's nest.

In his book, *Heavy Drinking: The Myth of Alcoholism as a Disease* (University of California, 1988), Herbert Fingarette "purposes that alcoholism is primarily a behavioral disorder, and that the very concept of 'alcoholism' is simplistic and arcane." ("Alcoholism: Is It a Sin After All?" *Christianity Today*, Februrary 3, 1989, p. 57.)

9         In critiquing an argument that homosexuals can claim victim status because of supposed "genetic" and psychological factors, Kenneth A. Myers, editor of *Genesis* magazine, wrote the following paragraph. Let it stand beside Mouw's comments and reveal how empty of biblical support remarks such as his really are. Myers writes:

> But what if one were to find a genetic or psychological predisposition toward racist behavior similar to factors that have been alleged . . . to "create" homosexuals? Would that mean that racists "can't help themselves," and so must be regarded as "normal" and accepted in society? . . . Why not? ("On Lobbies and Language," *Genesis*, February 12, 1990. p. 4.)

Although Myers is speaking of society as a whole, we see parallels in the evangelical community under the influence of "Christian" psychology. One wonders if we would be willing to say a professing believer, who is habitually and blatantly a racist, is really an "addictive victim" rather than one making a willful decision to hate? Why not? Do we not do it now for fornicators, adulterers and liars?

10      In a phone interview with *Christianity Today*, Fingarette made this fascinating comment:

> I just don't understand why any churches would go for the disease idea, except insofar as they are taken by the notion that we have to be enlightened and that seems to be the enlightened view. The disease approach denies the spiritual dimensions of the whole thing. People in the church may be afraid to take a different stand because it will be labeled antiscientific, antimodern, or old fashioned. I think that's all misguided. (Jim and Phyllis Alsdurf, "The 'Generic Disease,' " *Christianity Today*, December 9, 1988, pp. 36, 37.)

11 "Hollywood Update," *News From Youth with A Mission* (November, 1989), pp. 1, 2.

12 Oswald Chambers, "The Right Lines of Work," *My Utmost For His Highest* (Westwood: Dodd Mead and Company, Inc., 1963), p. 355.

# 7

# A Way Out of
# the Wilderness?

Recently someone asked me, "If you were raised in a
home where your father was alcoholic and you were abused
as a child, doesn't that make you a victim?" My answer was
brief but truthful. "I **was** raised in a home with an alcoholic
father," I said, and then I described one or two vivid recollec-
tions of childhood fears that flourished in that environment.
"But," I added, "Scripture never addresses me as a victim,
only as a sinner."

I know of no Scripture that directs me to search out past
hurts or to dwell upon them so that I might feel deeply how
much they have damaged my sense of self-worth. Scripture
never mentions such a backward probing as a route to progressive holiness or victory over abiding sin. Victimization
therapy is absent in God's instructions for either man's
redemption or for his sanctification.

When I was outside Christ, Scripture warned me of the
wrath to come. It condemned me as a rebel against the holy
God. Hell was my destiny. But Scripture also wooed me with
songs of God's redeeming love that could be mine in Christ. It
beckoned me to cast my vile and worthless self upon the mercies of the cross. It urged me with promises of hope to turn to

the living God from my dead and hateful idols. I was offered the glorious robes of Christ's righteousness in exchange for my own filthy rags of unrighteousness.

Now, as one who is in Christ, justified by faith through Christ, the Bible addresses me in intimate terms of endearment and encouragement and discipline. I am a new creation in Christ, dead to sin and all the ways of the old man. I am God's adopted son, freed from all spirits of fear. My body is now the temple of the Holy Spirit; my mind, Christ's. Sin no longer has dominion over me.

All of this Scripture tells me. But it is silent about victimization and apparently uninterested about any which occurred during my "formative" years.[1] It doesn't seem preoccupied with whether my self-esteem is appropriate. No matter how we squint our eyes or hold the book, we will not find those things there.

Just how much do Scripture and "Christian" psychology differ in this area? Let me give a few examples that will boldly frame the separation.

First and foremost is the scriptural insistence that from the beginning of our new life, we are to focus on Jesus Christ our Lord, not on the past. At all times, in all circumstances and on all occasions, **He** is to be the center of our life. He is the pearl of great price, the hidden treasure bringing great joy (Matthew 13:44,45). In Him are all the treasures of wisdom and knowledge (Colossians 2:3), and every thought is to be brought into captivity to His Lordship (2 Corinthians 10:5). Colossians 3:1-3 commands us to set our hearts and minds on things above where Christ is, not on earthly things.

The Bible tells us the old is gone, finished, dead and over—despite "Christian" psychology's insistence that we must probe ever so closely through the ashes and debris (2 Corinthians 5:17). We have been crucified with Christ. We have been buried with Him and raised to a new life so that we might present ourselves as alive to God and dead to sin (Romans 6:1-11).

Hebrews 3:1 tells us to fix our thoughts on Christ. Hebrews 12:2 charges us to fix, without wavering, our eyes upon Jesus, "the author and perfecter of our faith." Didn't our Lord Himself teach us to abide continuously in Him as a branch in the vine? Failure to do so would leave us withered, fruitless and joyless in our fellowship with the Father (John 15:1-11).

Neither these Scriptures nor any other I know of instructs us to rummage around among the dusty archives of our mind, uncovering and displaying our hurts and disappointments so that we might be closer to Jesus. To claim that the power of these past hidden or known victimizations is greater than the power of the cross, greater than the power of our risen and living Lord, or greater than the power of the indwelling Holy Spirit working within us (Ephesians 3:20) is an outright confession of unbelief.

J. I. Packer captured the heart of this issue when he wrote that those who truly know God "never brood on might-have-beens; they never think on the things they have missed, only on what they have gained."[2] If everything I had gained in life outside Christ can now be considered as a heap of manure, why should I brood over it and reflect upon its misfortunes, any more than I should delightfully recall my evil behavior? It is all manure.

There is a second scriptural problem with victim hunting. Victimization therapy demands that we painfully feel the hurts and disappointments that have supposedly damaged our self-esteem. We are not to deny them or even give them to Jesus. That would be considered a form of denial. Rather, we are to uncover them and feel emotionally the betrayal all over again. The process is often long and drawn out and self-absorbed—certainly delaying and even denying that present joy we are to experience in Christ.

## Joy in Christ

Present joy—the great theme of the New Testament, the exceeding great possession of those who are in Christ. "They have joy and comfort," wrote the Puritan Christopher Fowler, "that angels cannot give, and devils cannot take."[3] Alas, Fowler did not know that victimization thinking can accomplish what demons could not.

In a fallen world wrecked by sin and Satan, where laughter and happiness are always bracketed by depravity and death and fractured by malice and envy and godlessness, Christians, and Christians alone, have access to "joy inexpressible and full of glory" (1 Peter 1:8, NASB). Such was the joy of the believers Peter addressed in his first epistle. Even under the severest of trials they owned it because they believed in and loved Jesus. "Rejoice," Peter wrote them, "that you participate in the sufferings of Christ, so that you may be overjoyed when his glory is revealed" (1 Peter 4:13). Be joyful right now, so that you may have more joy later. Peter spoke from experience and practiced what he preached. (See Acts 5:29-42.)

Joy is what our Lord promised to all who would abide in Him and keep His commands. "I have told you this," he said, "so that my joy may be in you and that your joy may be complete" (John 15:11). Note that it is His joy that fills us, just as it is His love that constrains us. We cannot manufacture either one. Did I miss a disclaimer buried somewhere in John 15 that says I must first painfully realize the depth of my victimization before I can obey our Lord's gracious invitation and experience His joy in my obedience?

The epistle to the Philippians revolves around the theme of the believer's joy in Christ—even while tears and suffering for Christ are his everyday fare. Does not the same hold true for us today? When is the last time you heard a sermon on the believer's joy in Christ, circumstances notwithstanding? Are our circumstances and pressures so much greater than those of the New Testament world?

Why is it we hear so little about joy, and so much about hurting? Why do so many in Christ seem so ignorant of joy and even devoid of it? Perhaps it is time to look for the answer in such words as these from the pen of another Puritan, William Gurnall:

> The reason why so many poor souls have so little
> heat of joy in their hearts, is that they have so little
> light of the gospel knowledge in their mind. The fur-
> ther a soul stands from the light of truth, the fur-
> ther he must needs be from the heat of comfort.[4]

The Thessalonians were instructed to be joyful always
while giving "thanks in all circumstances, for this is God's
will for you in Christ Jesus" (1 Thessalonians 5:16,18). Evidently the Thessalonians took Paul's words to heart. Later,
he was to write the Corinthians that in the midst of severe
trial, and despite their extreme poverty, the "overflowing joy"
of this church "welled up in rich generosity" (2 Corinthians
8:2). How many of us could fit into such a picture today?

The supreme example of joy is our Lord Himself, as John
15:11 makes clear. "For the joy set before Him," the writer of
Hebrews informs us, Christ "endured the cross, scorning its
shame, and sat down at the right hand of the throne of God"
(Hebrews 12:2). William Morrice, in his fine little study, *Joy
in the New Testament*, writes that if Christ:

> . . . can justly be characterized as a "man of sorrows
> and acquainted with grief," he can with equal truth
> be described as "the man of joy." Shining right
> through his life—even at its darkest moments—
> there was a note of radiance and triumphant joy . . .
> joy was thus an ever-present reality in the life and
> work of Jesus.[5]

Even so, it is to be with us who have His joy within us. Our
joy in Christ is to nourish and nurture us even when we are
in deep pain, even when the pain threatens to overwhelm us.

Christ's joy in us is meant to transform us so that our
painful memories or present circumstances become opportu-
nities to glorify God and enjoy Him. It is a holy joy that
allows us to rejoice while sorrowing, experience His overcoming grace when weak and faint, that makes us triumphant

even when all those about us are claiming, "Hope is foolish and faith is useless."

"Unspeakable joy all day long and everyday was my happy experience," wrote Hudson Taylor in his latter years. "God, even my God, was a living bright reality, and all I had to do was joyful service."[6] When one considers this man's life in service to his Lord, this is a remarkable confession. But why should it be so remarkable? The Christ he followed is the same Christ we follow, isn't He? Do one hundred years make such a difference? Joy is the faithful companion for those who set their hearts and minds on Christ Jesus.

But the same cannot be said of those absorbed with their own victimization. It is difficult for anyone to focus on Christ when trying to trace out the forgotten, unnumbered and hurtful pathways of the past. It is impossible to truly rejoice and enjoy Christ when seeking to find and re-experience multiple painful events that brutalized one's fragile self-esteem.

"Forgetting what is behind," Paul wrote, "and straining toward what is ahead, I press on . . . ."

This is the heart of one who joys in Jesus.

## Counterfeit Joy

Could it be that for those who insist on dwelling on the past, there is another kind of joy—a grim, macabre, fleshly joy that bids them carry on? This is part of the darker side of victimization therapy. The flesh welcomes it; it loves to spread the blame and secretly relishes the scandal; it gladly welcomes anything that eases the intensity of our own disobedience and faithlessness. We revel in the opportunity to feel sorry for ourselves.

Of course, the intent of victimization therapy is to help free people from their past painful bondage and denials. But once the genie is free and visible, no one can guarantee it will disappear on command. It is amazing how many continue to keep their souls in a sad and doubting state over their victimization—even when supposedly free from its bondage, even after much therapy, even when it has supposedly been properly yielded to the Lord and put behind them. It is a wild and fleshy thing, though, this victim beast. Once uncaged, it lends its every cunning to avoid imprisonment.

J. I. Packer wrote insightfully along these lines. For most of us, he said, the disappointments and hurts of life matter greatly:

> We live with them as our "crosses" (so we call them). Constantly we find ourselves slipping into bitterness and apathy and gloom as we reflect on them, which we frequently do. . . . "Poor souls" our friends say of us, "how they've suffered"—and that is just what we feel about ourselves.[7]

The Puritan Thomas Brooks, in his classic work on counseling, *Precious Remedies Against Satan's Devices*, speaks of how Satan can keep believers in a constant state of doubt and guilt and fear:

> . . . by causing them to be still pouring and musing upon their sin, to mind their sins more than their Savior; yea, so to mind their sins as to forget, yea to neglect their Savior.[8]

Today we must add a corollary to his comment: Satan keeps believers in a joyless and depressing and bitter state "by causing them to be still pouring and musing upon [the sins others have committed against them]; to mind the [sins of others against them] more than their Savior; yea, so to mind [the sins of others against them] as to forget, yea, to neglect their Savior."

At one youth retreat, a young lady stood up during a question and answer period and told the speaker she had been molested as a child. Did she not have a right to feel bitter and angry whenever she thought of the person that did it, she tearfully demanded?

The speaker's reply caught us all by surprise. "Why," he asked, "are you letting Satan rob you of your joy in Christ?" The young woman did not know how to answer. Now, what she said to the speaker was not new to the group. They knew her and knew what had happened to her, and she was loved and respected by them. She had been counseled over the incident. She even knew the answer to her own question. Yet she was still musing over her victimization. By bringing up the incident once again, she was reminding us, "See how I continue to suffer," and extracting from all her friends one more fix of sympathy.

Victimization opens us up to this sorrowing view of self. To forgive and not to forget (in a scriptural sense) is not to forgive at all. Rather, it is to ignore what Paul wrote, "Forgetting what is behind . . . ."

I can understand unbelievers opening their arms. They hope to hide their culpability in such an embrace. But how can we who stand before the cross embrace so carnal and faithless a concept as this? When I consider the hurts and disappointments of my life, it is not those inflicted upon me that cause my heart to anguish. No, rather it is my sins against others and my Lord—oh, especially against my Lord—that bring me shame and pain. I would despair beyond hope were it not for the grace of my God and Savior, Jesus Christ. Satan would have me mind my sins into all eternity. But Jesus has told me to forget what is behind and press forward for the prize of the high calling of God in Himself. Joyfully and gratefully I do so!

## Bitterness Toward the Cross

One last fault of victimization therapy needs to be discussed. It gives birth to a brooding mood that mutters bitter words at the cross. The unrelenting insistence on entering into our victimized past to feel deeply the pain of our betrayal and the mangling of our self-esteem carries the unspoken demand that Jesus "owes" us the cross and much more.

Victimization shifts the emphasis from the pain and shame Christ endured for me, to the burden of pain and shame and bondage I have had to bear because of what others have done to me. Thus even God is taken hostage by our past.

How subtle is this sin! Let us consider a slightly edited rendering of Luke 9:59-61, a rendering that would incorporate the victimization concept into Christ's call to obedience:

> The Lord said to one man, "Follow me."
>
> But the man replied: "Lord, first let me go back and analyze my childhood. Bad and harmful things were done to me then. My family failed to affirm me properly. Let me go back and again feel deeply the hurts and disappointments I experienced. Only then can I forgive those who inflicted them upon me. Only then can I overcome my dysfunctional behavior. Only then will I be able to develop an appropriate self-esteem. Only then can I truly ask your forgiveness. Only then, Lord, will I be free to follow you."
>
> Jesus replied: "Let the dead bury their own dead, but you go and proclaim the kingdom of God. No one who puts his hand to the plow and looks back is fit for the kingdom of God."

Is my edited version unfair? Perhaps. Then let me quote the unedited text of Colossians 2:20: "Since you died with Christ to the basic principles of this world, why as though you still belong to it, do you submit to its rules?"

## The Clarity of Scripture

There is a glorious simplicity about the Scriptures, an unpretentious directness that makes glad the heart of all who place themselves at their command. There is a simplicity that leaves little room for sophistry and rationalization. Oh, there are many deep things that cause us to ponder long and intensely. Again and again we must come back to drink from its pure depths with prayer and meditation. Yet there is an inescapable simplicity that makes crystal clear the will and intent of God regarding man—both saved and lost.

For example, listen to 1 John 4:20: "If anyone says, 'I love God,' yet hates his brother, he is a liar." That is about as direct and simple as one could ask. Scripture is very much this way in speaking to our motives and behavior. Over and over again, it simply tells the believer to "avoid sexual immorality," or "be holy because I am holy," or "flee the evil desires of youth," or "love one another deeply from the heart."

When the Holy Spirit addresses us in this simple manner, three things are unmistakably clear:

1. We know what is being asked of us. We know how God wants us to live (John 13:34). There may be gray areas and we may have our freedoms in Christ, but even these are to be informed by the attitude that Christ commanded in pursuing our redemption (Philippians 2:5-8).

2. We want to obey the things the Spirit is commanding us to do, because we have a new heart that loves righteousness and loves God. It is to those who have been made new in Christ that God entrusts the ministry of reconciliation (2 Corinthians 5:17ff). It is those who have God's Spirit who focus their hearts and minds on what the Spirit desires (Romans 8:5). Our Lord told us that if we loved Him we would obey His commands and that "whoever has my commands and obeys them, he is the one who loves me" (John 14:15,21).

We may struggle with the flesh; it may beg, plead, demand and rage to be uncrucified, and we may, to our shame and horror, yield to its evil desires in a time of unfaithfulness; but the believer longs in his new heart to obey his Lord and be empowered by the Holy Spirit to mortify his flesh. He bends all his strength in cooperation (Colossians 1:29; 2 Corinthians 7:1).

3. We have been given the means by which we can obey God. For God the Holy Spirit is in us working God's will in us "to act according to His good purpose" (Philippians 2:13).

The Spirit guides us "into all truth," taking what is from Christ and making it ours (John 16:13-15). This is doubly true in regard to the Scriptures, so that we might have hope and be trained for righteousness and "equipped for every good work" (Romans 15:4; 2 Timothy 3:16,17). In addition, Christ, through the Spirit, has given us manifold gifts and gifted men, in order that we might be prepared for service, strengthened in our unity and brought to the proper maturity that becomes children of the King (Ephesians 4:11-13; 1 Peter 4:10,11).

With the gifts come the promises, promises that sweep away all obscurity about God's love. Promises that allow us to "participate in the divine nature and escape the corruption in the world caused by evil desires" (2 Peter 1:4). We have His promise of protection from the evil one (1 John 5:18; 2 Thessalonians 3:3) and His promise to complete the "good work" he has begun in us (Philippians 1:6). We have His promise of faithfulness that will keep us blameless for the coming of our Lord Jesus (1 Thessalonians 5:23,24) and we have the promise of His power working within us "to do immeasurably more than we ask or imagine" (Ephesians 3:20).

All this is ours. Great promises from the mouth of our God who is faithful and will do it, and who will not let Himself be defamed before an unbelieving world nor yield His "glory to another" (Isaiah 48:11). It is He who promises that we are never "tempted beyond what [we] can bear." He is the One who has promised that with the temptation He "will also provide a way out so that [we] can stand up under it" (1 Corinthians 10:13). Listen to the One who promised that if He "did not spare his own Son, but gave him up for all of us— how will he not also, along with him, graciously give us all things?" (Romans 8:32).

Given all of this, is there a basis in Scripture for saying that the "bad conditioning" I received in growing up can nullify the promises and power of God's grace? Is there a scriptural basis to support a Christian psychologist's assertion to the wife of a pastor who committed adultery, that it wouldn't have mattered if he had had many wives because he was "destined" to do what he did because of his upbringing? Dare we call such a conclusion anything else but a denial of God's promises?

I am enjoined to believe God's Word and to lean uninhibitedly upon the promised mercies and strengths. The promises of God and my response to them are never contingent upon a works process that is in essence a combination of psychoanalysis and emotional catharsis. Psychoanalysis is not to precede obedience and catharsis is not to precede forgiveness.

## Does God Tease Us with His Promises?

If our "victimization" destines us to certain sinful behavior, then one is tempted to think that God teases us with His promises. To command us not to receive the grace of God in vain (2 Corinthians 6:1) and to perfect "holiness out of reverence for God," turning therefore from "everything that contaminates body and spirit" (2 Corinthians 7:1), is a mean-spirited thing to do if we cannot obey because we are slaves to our past. God told the Corinthians they would not be tempted beyond what they were able to endure (1 Corinthians 10:13). Is this not an act of meanness if any of them were like the young lady who was constantly bed-hopping because she was supposedly trying to get back at her father for neglecting her?

James details a vastly different understanding of temptation (and overcoming it) than the idea of engaging in debauched activities in an attempt to overcome feelings of past rejection. For he tells us we are tempted by our own "evil desires," which drag us away and entice us. "Then," James writes, "after desire has conceived, it gives birth to sin; and sin, when it is full-grown, gives birth to death" (James 1:14,15).

Yes, people can be in bondage to sin—unbelievers continuously and completely. But the cross breaks that enslavement. Sin's dominion is ended and the demons have been defeated (Colossians 2:10-15). This is the great liberating message of the New Testament. To deny this is to deny the Scriptures and the legitimacy of the proclamation of the church over the last two thousand years.

The reason people are in bondage to sin is not because of victimization or low self-esteem. Ephesians 4:19 says they are the way they are because they have "lost all sensitivity" (toward God) and thus "have given themselves over to sensuality so as to indulge in every kind of impurity with a continual lust for more." Here we have true culpability!

When a Christian reverts to sinful behavior, he is in essence denying his death; he is returning to a form of self-idolatry. Why then is it unreasonable that counseling for such a believer should begin at Calvary and not in the recapitulations of victimization? Should he not be confronted with the Word of God to expose the hidden motives of idolatry within his heart (Hebrews 4:12), rather than be informed he has been psychologically maimed by his parents and thus has an inadequate self-esteem?

What we are wrestling over in all of this is the question of ultimate authority. Whom do we believe, whom do we follow? Authority can't be shared in this matter. We can't be quoting 1 Corinthians 10:13 to people while at the same time telling them they were destined to commit adultery because they were victimized as children. We are not dealing with scriptural paradoxes here, but conflicting world views—one divine, the other secular. Contradictions of this nature cannot be integrated.

Victimization therapy ultimately diminishes the impact and significance of the cross of our Lord. Even if Scripture **seems** to be woven into the fabric of victimization therapy, reliance is not on the power and promise of God's Word to heal or bring fruits of repentance. The therapy is supposed to do the work. While such therapy may not deny that we are justified by Christ's work on the cross, it limits the cross's power to that arena. It claims real sanctification occurs only through victimization therapy.

Yet to downgrade the cross is frightening, for it alone is the true means of our sanctification. Martin Lloyd-Jones has expressed this truth as well as anyone I know:

> You do not say the cross is only about justification, or the cross is only about conversion and that then we leave that and go to higher reaches. . . . No, the cross governs sanctification. It is the mightiest argument for sanctification.[9]

It is at the cross that the old is exchanged for the new, the disfiguring yoke of sin replaced by the gentle and gracious yoke of Jesus. It is at the cross that the Holy Spirit is poured into our hearts as evidence of God's amazing love (Romans 5:5). It is at the cross that the power of God is freed to work in us to do His will and good purpose, working within us to do far more than we can think or imagine (Ephesians 3:20).

All of this speaks of a new heart, a new purpose, a new meaning, a new calling, a new mind and, most of all, a new love, an all-consuming passion for Christ and His glory. How can we say a man is destined to commit adultery because of his childhood victimization? God help us if this is the direction we are heading. Pity the Christian who is happy to trade the cross for such a self-excusing, self-preoccupied state of mind!

Victimization therapy is not so much a spiritual process achieving spiritual goals by spiritual means as it is a rationalistic process seeking behavioral goals and using humanistic means. It is the exact reverse of what Paul discusses in 1 Corinthians 2:9-16. In these verses, the apostle explains how we receive insight and wisdom from the Holy Spirit "not in words taught us by human wisdom but in words taught by the Spirit, expressing spiritual truths in spiritual words" (1 Corinthians 2:13). They are taught to us so that we can "understand what God has freely given us." What enormous amounts of grace there are in these words!

How can victimization counseling encourage confidence in the preaching and teaching of the Word of God? Or in the expectations of believing prayer? Or in the efficacy of abiding in Christ, or truly resting, as the believer ought to, upon the awesome experiential knowledge that "I can do everything through him who gives me strength" (Philippians 4:13)?

In a small book titled *Humility*, Andrew Murray wrote these words:

> Let us study the character of Christ until our souls are filled with love and admiration of his lowliness. And let us believe that, when we are broken down under a sense of pride, and our impotence to cast it out, Jesus Christ Himself will come in to impart this grace to us, as a part of his wondrous life within us.[10]

Could this simple approach be the way out of our psychological wilderness?

There is a great mystery, I admit, in the words, "Christ in you, the hope of glory." Is anyone still willing to trust so simple a foundation as this? "When the Son of Man comes," Jesus asked, "will he find faith on the earth?" (Luke 18:8.)

Evangelical Christianity is in serious trouble. We have joined ourselves to rationalism. We wipe our mouths and refuse to admit we have done anything wrong. And our sin is that much greater because we have clothed our humanism in Christian garb and claim certainty for it.

Shortly before he died, Francis Schaeffer penned these words:

> *To accommodate to the world spirit about us in our age is the most gross form of worldliness in the proper definition of the word.* And unhappily today we must say that in general the evangelical establishment has been accommodating to the form of

the world spirit as it finds expression in our day . . .
in the most basic sense, the evangelical establishment has become deeply worldly.[11] (Emphasis his.)

Schaeffer's words are more germane today than when he
first wrote them. And the pace accelerates. "Christian" psychology, with its victimization counseling methodology drawn
straight from humanistic presuppositions, has become the
most obvious and open expression of this accommodating
worldliness.

---

## Notes

1      Some psychologists seek to use Exodus 34:7, "Yet he
does not leave the guilty unpunished; he punishes the
children and their children for the sins of the fathers to
the third and fourth generation," as scriptural support for
children following in the footsteps of their parents' addictive or abusive behavior.

But in Ezekiel 18 God abrogates this "curse" for the
son who repents and turns from following his Father's
wicked behavior. "The soul who sins is the one who will
die. The son will not share the guilt of the father, nor will
the father share the guilt of the son" (vs. 20). Likewise,
the New Testament promise that the one who comes to
Christ has been freed from sin's dominion simply cannot
be denied without saying Scripture is wrong.

2    J. I. Packer, *Knowing God* (Downers Grove: Intervarsity
Press, 1973), p. 21.

3    *The Golden Treasury of Puritan Quotations*, compiled by
I. D. E. Thomas (Chicago: Moody Press, 1975), p. 159.

4    *Ibid.*, p. 158.

5  William Morrice, *Joy in the New Testament* (Grand Rapids: William B. Eerdmans Publishing Company, 1985), p. 86.

6     This quote is found in John Piper's *Desiring God*, p. 223. Hudson Taylor also made the remarkable statement that he never made a sacrifice. David Livingstone made a like confession. One can only surmise what such men might think of our present-day preoccupation with victimization and self-esteem.

7  Packer, *Knowing God, op. cit.*, p. 20.

8  Thomas Brooks, *Precious Remedies Against Satan's Devices* (London: The Banner of Truth Trust, 1968), p. 142.

9  Martyn Lloyd-Jones, *The Cross* (Westchester: Crossway Books, 1986), p. 213.

10  Andrew Murray, *Humility* (Fort Washington, PA: Christian Literature Crusade, 1974), p. 17.

11  Francis A. Schaeffer, *The Great Evangelical Disaster* (Westchester: Crossway Books, 1984), p. 142.

# 8

# Who Is To Be the Master?

The sophisticated way in which "Christian" psychology fends off its critics and justifies its pathological interpretation of man brings to mind a conversation a young girl named Alice once had with a cosmopolitan old rotten egg named Humpty Dumpty.

They were discussing how many "unbirthday" presents one could receive. Humpty Dumpty was grandly declaring "that there are three hundred and sixty-four days when you might get unbirthday presents—"

"Certainly," said Alice.

"And only *one* for birthday presents, you know. There's glory for you!"

"I don't know what you mean by 'glory,' " Alice said.

Humpty Dumpty smiled contemptuously. "Of course you don't—till I tell you. I meant 'there's a nice knock-down argument for you!' "

"But 'glory' doesn't mean 'a nice knock-down argument,' " Alice objected.

> "When *I* use a word," Humpty Dumpty said, in
> a rather scornful tone, "it means just what I choose
> it to mean—neither more nor less."
> "The question is," said Alice, "whether you *can*
> make words mean different things."
> "The question is," said Humpty Dumpty, "which
> is to be the master—that's all."[1] (Emphasis in origi-
> nal.)

While I can't agree with Humpty Dumpty's lexicography,
I can agree with his final statement: ". . . which is to be the
master—that's all." That's the question. Who is to be the
master? Nowhere is this question more relevant than in the
current discussion.

One noted Christian psychologist, known for his inner
healing techniques, believes "we do not need to be afraid of
anything helpful which comes through" avenues of "generalized" grace, because these, too, are gifts from God. While this
gentleman graciously admits these "discovered" truths are
not to be considered "on the same level as God's revealed
truth," nonetheless he considers them God's truths. Therefore
he insists, "As Christians, we are required by God to use
every gift He has given us for His glory and for human
good."[2]

No one would disagree with this last thought. But, while
in theory "Christian" psychology may say "discovered" truth
is not on the same level as revealed truth, in practice the dis-
tinction evaporates. In fact, "discovered" truth has a way of
becoming the only functional truth. We end up being captured by the merely theoretical, accepting a conception of
reality as if it were reality.

This was brought sharply to my attention by an article in
the *Los Angeles Times*. The author, Michael Schrage, takes
environmental scientists to task for greatly overstating their
case for global warming. The author argues that because our
data is woefully incomplete and our understanding of the
basic forces involved so limited, it is impossible to claim that
"the scientific models of global warming, presently being

touted in the media," are truly hard scientific fact. "Too many scientists," the author writes, "have fallen in love with their models," a situation that threatens to undermine the credibility of the scientists themselves.[3]

Schrage's article offers an excellent illustration on how we can exaggerate our expertise under the aegis of "discovered" truth. This is a message "Christian" psychology desperately needs to hear. Christian psychologists have been less than modest in trying to present psychology as science. The use of the axiom "all truth is God's truth" is only a polite way of saying, "Psychology is to be trusted because it is truly science." At many points "Christian" psychology has overstated its case, as well as overstepped the limits of Scripture.

How, for instance, does one show scientifically that we have an unconscious mind, ominously bubbling with hurts and disappointments and bad conditioning—a brooding, subterranean master that dictates to and imprisons our will? In fact, a master so powerful that even the new man in Christ and the indwelling Holy Spirit cannot subdue it. Is this science? It certainly isn't Scripture!

What we have in "Christian" psychology is the exaltation of theory and subjectivism to the podium of objective, scientific truth. This "truth" is then held up alongside Scripture and used with the same authority as Scripture when counseling the wayward.

To claim that psychology can heal the heart as one would use medical science to heal the body is to make a claim that cannot be proven. If I have a broken leg, I can factually prove the break, where it is located, how to repair it and whether the cure is successful and lasting. Can anyone claim the same certainty for the "truths" of psychology?

Let's do a comparison. If I bring together such Scriptures as Romans 13:14, James 1:14,15 and 4:1-5, Galatians 5:16-21 and 6:7,8, and 1 Thessalonians 4:3-8, I could give you a clear, biblical explanation on why a man might commit adultery. It would be factual and true. God's revelation in Scripture cannot be anything less.

I could even say that I don't have to look elsewhere for an explanation. I can rightfully approach that man and, using Scripture, call him to repentance. I can also confidently say that if he does repent and acknowledge Jesus as Lord, he can stop his behavior. All of this I can confidently say because God's revealed truth says so.

But if you tell me the same man commits adultery because he is trying to prove his manhood, that he is suffering from an unconquerable compulsion brought on by a father who damaged his self-esteem as a child, I say first that "Christian" psychology should blush to claim any Scriptural commendation for such an analysis. Second, I say that you are giving me unadulterated conjecture based upon a particular theory of personality development that is no more scientific than "a coin toss," to use Mr. Schrage's words again.[4]

To claim that victimization therapy, built upon a pathological view of man, is truly science, that it is a part of God's truth, uncovered by diligently sorting and sifting through the unlabeled "goodies" of generalized revelation, is to come dangerously close to what the ancient Greeks called *hubris*—an overweening pride in one's wisdom and abilities that would move the gods to jealousy and retribution. We may say we can use any knowledge from the world we want as long as it doesn't violate the guidelines of Scripture, but this is watery gruel indeed when one considers how elastic those guidelines have proved to be.

## Is the Church the Problem?

Perhaps we should not be so surprised to discover, all truth being what it is and "Christian" psychology being master of its own semantics, that the real problem is not with the arcane thinking of "Christian" psychology but rather with the church, its leaders and their outdated loyalties to the Bible.

Too often I read that the church has failed to meet the "needs" of its people. It is the church that has been insensitive to inherited, sinful bondage. It is the church that has been simplistic in its approach to the complexities of human problems and addictions, offering only "simple-minded spiritual solutions" to problems that are as much physical and psychological as they are spiritual. Too often I hear the church has done more harm than good with its simplistic "reminders of God's love and exhortations to meditate on Jesus' care." Too often the church, bound by rigid theology and dated pietistic formulas, has failed to realize that it can take a great deal of effort and "people helping us in complicated and professional ways to undo the power of sin in our lives."

Are we really to believe that for two thousand years God's faithful servants have misinterpreted His revelation on how to preach the Gospel to the lost, guide in the sanctification of His people, encourage the weak, and discipline those in sin? Has Christ's body, with all its faults and failures, become so estranged from its Lord that He has had no choice but to reveal His truth through such servants as Freud and Maslow and Fromm and Rogers? Are we to believe their "discovered" truths are now to be trusted more than the Scriptures?

Or is the waving of such a tattered banner as "all truth is God's truth" simply an admission that Scripture does not support "Christian" psychology?[5] Perhaps this is why "Christian" psychology is so quick to separate the spiritual from the psychological—each having its own method of interpreting reality, its own method of treatment, its own source of truth.

The truth is, "Christian" psychology is staking out a claim as a new revelation worthy to stand beside Scripture, possessing equal authority and even, at times, superseding it. Certainty is being attributed to human conjecture and Scripture is being mocked.

Psychology is the only discipline I know that creates its own clientele by inventing its own diseases. Not only does it invent them; it also defines them, determines who has caught them and creates the cure—all in the same breath. Thus we find we are "relationally dysfunctional" or "diseased" or "addicted" or the latest catch-all, "codependent." The latter one truly upsets me. It epitomizes much that I have been trying to articulate, and I will have much to say about it in the next chapter.

## Turning Away from Scripture

The fundamental error of "Christian" psychology is that it turns away from the authority of Scripture. It attempts to ground the believer's walk, not in faith in Christ, but rather in knowledge. It is a modern version of gnosticism. It teaches that Christians struggle and fail to master sin not because they cherish sin more than their Lord, nor because of willful disobedience or a lack of faith, but because of human ignorance.

This ignorance has shaped the believer's destiny and has kept him sinning over and over again, no matter how much prayer and Bible study and repentance have been practiced. Only when our ignorance is removed can the Holy Spirit begin to off-set the bondage, says psychology—and only psychology can remove this ignorance. Whether it is in small group settings or one-to-one with a professional counselor, it doesn't matter. What matters is the method of therapy and perhaps the length.

But does Scripture support this gnostic interpretation of our sinfulness or the prescribed method for our cure? Consider, for example, David's adultery. God did not send Nathan to David to encourage him to get into victimization therapy. Nathan did not tell David that denial of his past hurts had led him into sin. Nor did he point the king toward a 12-step group for the sexually addicted. God seemed unconcerned with what prompted David to do what he did. But, He was very concerned that David committed adultery when he knew it violated God's' law, and He was concerned about what David's actions signified. (See 2 Samuel 12:1-10.) David was not considered a victim unconsciously responding to unhealed memories—and neither was Bathsheba.

God indicted David for despising Him and causing His name to be held in contempt. Through Nathan, God reminded David how gracious and good He had been to David. In fact, had the king wanted more, God would have given it. Instead, David deliberately **chose** to hold all that God had given him in contempt and to go after what he wanted.

The point of rehearsing David's sin is to emphasize that, considering God's close and unique relationship with David, God expected David to be faithful. Further, He knew that he could be faithful.

How much more so should it be for us who have wept before the cross and experienced its cleansing power! Nowhere, nowhere does the New Testament teach that a person filled with the Holy Spirit will, despite all his Spirit-prompted efforts to obey his Lord, remain in unrelieved bondage to sinful behavior. Nowhere does Scripture teach that year after year such a person will live a defeated Christian life, robbed of his joy in Christ, because of past victimizations.[6] Anyone who thinks Scripture teaches that should sit down and read it again.

More and more, it is not the Word of God that binds our hearts and minds in common unity, but rather our particular "dysfunction" or "addiction" or "need." With increasing frequency, the church is being fragmented into small groups centered on the group's common problem and often organized around the 12-step method adapted from Alcoholics Anonymous. We share our problems, we share our feelings, we share our victimizations, and we share our sinful lusts—in fact, we almost glory in these things. The result is a dependent elitism. One comes to believe that only the others in the group can really understand him or her. "Only those in my group know what I suffer, struggle with, hurt over."

## Five Dangers of Support Groups

Of course, the idea behind such groups can serve a good purpose. It is good to know that others of like background have overcome temptation and are there to encourage us. But the dangers inherent in such groupings are many and detrimental to the church. Let me list five such dangers.

1. Because group identity is so strong, there is little real identification with the rest of the church or with its mission. In fact, one sees the mission of the church as meeting one's own particular need, which is helping to control one's problem and work through the pain it causes.

2. There is little deep fellowship with, or ministry to, other believers outside the "identity" group. Only the group can provide the unique sympathy craved.

3. Dependence on the group is usually so great that if one is separated from it for any length of time, one's Christian walk begins to deteriorate.

4. Because the group's center is the group's common problem and the methodology designed to control the problem, there never develops the confidence in Christ's faithfulness, which allows one to experience the reality of His sufficiency and power. Instead, sufficiency and power flow from the group and the group's methodology.

5. One's relation with Christ becomes self-centered. It always focuses on one's problem and how one can use Christ to keep it under control. This sabotages a healthy relationship of absolute dependence on Christ. One never completely accepts Jesus as his Lord of Glory, his only hope of glory and himself as a servant of others for Christ's sake (2 Corinthians 4:5). The very nature of the group limits one's ability to move toward bringing every thought captive to Christ, where one's every longing is to see Christ face to face, where one's every work is to glorify and exalt Christ alone and one's greatest joy is fellowship with Christ.

It is sad to note how often those who get into these groups never seem to get beyond their problem. They never seem to get their focus on Christ. They are always pondering their victimization or the problems stemming from it. They continue to identify themselves as a "recovering" something or other, still working through their feelings. In other words, they remain self-focused.

Such fragmenting of believers is unbiblical. All such groupings ultimately teach a deficient understanding of Christ and our new life in Him. The glory of the Christian's calling, the whole purpose of his or her life in Christ, is to exalt Christ wholeheartedly, worship Him and imitate Him with great joy. It is not to create a "life that is under control" or "a behavior that works."

Both Scripture and personal experience teach me that believers are not to center their lives around any particular sin or the memory of it or the threat of it. Nor are they to fellowship on the basis of any sin. But that is exactly what groups modeled on AA do. One must never forget one's problem or escape its shadow. The bondage continues despite Christ. The great liberty that is ours in Christ is never experienced (Romans 6:14), nor is the Great Liberator ever trusted as He desires (Hebrews 4:14-16). What is trusted and practiced is the method itself.

The Christian's growing reliance on such methods as the 12-step program is a terrible admission about our lack of reliance on the reality and power of our Lord Jesus. The words of C. S. Lewis echo hauntingly from the past to question our fading and tattered evangelical faith. "For I am not sure, after all," he wrote:

> . . . whether one of the causes of our weak faith is not a secret wish that our faith should not be very strong. Is there some reservation in our minds? Some fear of what it might be like if our religion became quite real? I hope not. God help us all, and forgive us.[7]

### A Better Way

Scripture offers us a far more excellent way, and a far more exciting way, than any 12-step method. In 1 Corinthians 6:9-11, Paul lists many sinful behaviors that once characterized the Corinthians. Some had been sexually promiscuous. Others had been adulterers, male prostitutes and homosexuals. Still others had been idolaters, thieves, greedy money-grubbers, drunkards, slanderers and swindlers.

Yet concerning this group Paul makes one of the most beautiful statements found anywhere in the Scriptures. Beautiful, you see, because it includes me. This is what he writes: "And that is what some of you **were**." What an awesome statement! "You **were**"—past tense, a big past tense. You **were** that but you **are not** that anymore. What a glorious declaration of deliverance! Can you believe it? But Paul doesn't stop there. He goes on to say, "But you were washed, you were sanctified, you were justified in the name of the Lord Jesus Christ and by the Spirit of God." Cleaned up, made straight and set free.

Not only were they saved, but the Holy Spirit was among them and in them, bringing them all together in one place. The unheard of was happening. There, together in the same house, were a Jew and ex-idolater. With them were an ex-homosexual slave and a one-eyed ex-thief who used to fornicate with the prostitutes of Aphrodite's temple. But no more. There they were, sitting side by side listening to Paul preach, "Jesus is Lord to the glory of God the Father," and nodding their heads in agreement, radiating a joy inexpressible and full of glory. Imagine it if you will. But remember this—it wasn't imaginary.

Also, imagine this if you will. The one thing you don't read of the Corinthians doing, even after many behaved carnally, even after Satan moved in with his "super-apostles" and Paul had to apply strong disciplinary measures—the one thing you don't find them doing is breaking up into small groups each according to each one's past, sinful "addiction." In fact, no present, sinful addiction was tolerated.

The ex-drunkards didn't get off by themselves because only other ex-drunkards could understand their hurts and disappointments and struggles. Nor did the ex-homosexuals, ex-thieves, ex-prostitutes, ex-swindlers or ex-anybody. Their fellowship was not in what they had been or what had been done to them. It was centered in Jesus Christ. They had been washed, sanctified and justified "in the name of the Lord Jesus Christ and by the Spirit of our God."

Now they could forget what was behind because they shared a common present and future—Jesus Christ and His kingdom. So they mingled—swindlers and whores, the greedy and the idolaters—ministering God's grace to one another, irrespective of their past, as only men and women saved by grace can do. They were not "recovering" victims of any stripe. Instead, they were the children of God, learning to bring glory to Him in all they said and did and learning to imitate their heavenly Father by focusing exclusively on their elder brother Jesus, the author and perfecter of their faith. And wonder of wonders, it worked. Warts and all, it worked!

If I may be forgiven for using a cliché, "It doesn't get any better than this." Those words certainly fit better with the redeemed of God than in a beer ad.

Is our situation really so different today that it wouldn't work for us, too?

---

## Notes

1   Lewis Carroll, *Alice's Adventure in Wonderland* (New York: Liverwright, Inc., Publishers, ND), pp. 246, 247.

2   David A. Seamands, *Healing Grace* (Wheaton: Victor Books, 1988), pp. 187-189.

3   Michael Schrage, "Why Beauty of Scientific Models is often Only Skin Deep," *Los Angeles Times* (December 21, 1989), pp. D-1,7.

4   *Ibid.*, p. 7.

5   Let me relate just two examples:

A. Minirth and Meier, in their book, *Happiness Is A Choice* (Baker Book House, 1978), make the following interpretation:

> Jeremiah 17:9 is the key to Christian psychiatry: "The Heart is deceitful above all things, and desperately wicked, who can know it?" The prophet Jeremiah is saying that we humans cannot fathom or comprehend how desperately sinful and deceitful our heart is—our unconscious motives, conflicts, drives, emotions, and thoughts (p. 97).

Without so much as an explanation, we find that Jeremiah is talking about the "unconscious" mind. This is a cavalier assumption that ignores that the heart in Old Testament usage refers to all that man is within, including his reason and will. It is not referring to the Freudian "unconscious" mind; one has to believe in that concept to find it in this Scripture.

They give a similar twist to Proverbs 11:14 ("Where there is no guidance, the people fall [NIV, "nation falls"], but in an abundance of counselors there is victory.") This proverb refers to the fate of a nation that lacks wise and humble political leadership. But notice what Minirth and Meier do with it:

> Some people (especially in the lower middle-class) poke fun at getting professional counseling . . . but this ridicule is the product of their own naiveté and defensiveness. Getting guidance from a knowledgeable Christian pastor or professional counselor can bring about victory over life's seemingly overwhelming stresses. **To obtain and apply to one's life good-quality Christian psychotherapy is synonymous with discipleship** (p. 98, emphasis added).

What a fascinating conclusion this last sentence contains! A proverb meant to speak to the issue of the quality of political leadership becomes a justification for "Christian" psychiatric counseling, and psychiatric counseling (i.e., psychotherapy) becomes equated with discipleship. One can only wonder if Solomon knew what he was endorsing?

B. Jan Frank, in her book, *A Door of Hope* (Here's Life Publishers, 1987), interprets the parable of the Wheat and Tares (Matthew 13) "as **a beautiful illustration of what happens to us as victims** . . ." (p 158, emphasis added). Some people plant good seeds into little children's lives, she writes, and this is the wheat. The tares are the lies Satan plants in little children's hearts that they are worthless or no good or that God doesn't love them. These lies are planted at stressful moments in the child's heart, such as when a molestation occurs. As one grows up, Satan reinforces these lies. "All of these lies are planted by the enemy," she writes, "to affect our fruitfulness for God" (p. 159). But when we grow up we need to "expose" and root out and replace with God's Word these Satanic lies we have been believing "even on a sub-conscious level," lies that cause one to feel depressed, guilty, angry and even suicidal.

It can be difficult to critique this type of eisegesis because it is done in such an emotional context. In addition, Frank claims the Holy Spirit showed her this interpretation. But one has to ask why our Lord bothered giving an interpretation to this parable at all. Dealing with "painful" past circumstances does not give us a mandate to use God's Word in a self-serving manner so that we might justify our methodologies.

One could write a thick book just on how "Christian" psychologists bend and loop and twist Scripture to meet the configurations of their presuppositions and resultant methodologies.

6 David Seamands makes just such an assertion in an interview with *Christianity Today*. Commenting on

Charles Wesley's words, "He breaks the power of cancelled sin, he sets the prisoner free" (from the hymn "O for a Thousand Tongues"), Seamands is quoted as saying:

> The point is that it's possible to have sin cancelled and for it still to have power over you. People can accept Christ, be on their way to heaven, and yet there's hurt and sin in the past that has power over them. It's got to be broken, and if it's not broken they cannot live faithfully.

Seamands then defends the inner healing of memories, not the cross or the Holy Spirit, as the appropriate way to accomplish this. ("Underfire," *Christianity Today*, September 18, 1987, p. 21.) Seamands, of course, is not unique among "Christian" psychologists in his position. In a way, he spoke for just about all of "Christian" psychology.

7  C. S. Lewis, *Christian Reflections* (Walter Hooper, ed. Grand Rapids: William B. Eerdmans Publishing Company, 1967), p. 43.

# 9

# The Wrong Answers, the Wrong Questions

Not too long ago, a friend had a conversation with a psychologist who believes wholeheartedly that "before we'll see how sinful we are as a self-protective agent, we must first feel how disappointed we are as a vulnerable victim." When pressed, the psychologist admitted he couldn't reconcile his victimization theology with Scripture, but said he believed in it anyway. On another occasion, this psychologist proclaimed that today's Christians have a leg up on Christians of the past because of "Christian" psychology.

Let us suppose that this psychologist is in tune with reality. If he is right, then we need to take a closer look at the statement quoted above. If he is right, we should appreciate remarks like the one that follows from the writings of David Seamands, who believes it is impossible to appropriate God's grace without the "inner healing" of past victimizations:

> God's care cannot be felt without a deep inner reprogramming of all the bad conditioning that has been put into them by parents and family and teachers and preachers and the church.[1]

Let us suppose "Christian" psychology is right, that we must go through this form of therapy before we can be free to respond to God's grace in the way God desires. Let's make this our starting point. Where does this road lead us?

If "Christian" psychology is right about the reason for our sinful behavior, and if victimization therapy is the correct way to cure it, and if the concept and methodology are not readily discernible in Scripture, then we must conclude that not only are we blameless for our failure to obey God, but that the blame must be laid at the feet of God Himself!

If "Christian" psychology is right, then until its recent discovery Christians lacked the wherewithal to understand and overcome the wrong choices to which they were addicted.

Whom can we hold responsible for this but God? And we must ask: How could He have been so lax? How could He have been so indifferent to His people's needs? Did He not realize they were hurting and disappointed and needed to work through their relational dysfunctions? How could He have been so calloused as to demand rejoicing and thanksgiving in every circumstance and obedience based on love, yet know that such was not possible without the insights of "Christian" psychology?

Worse, how could He have inspired the apostle Peter to write, "His divine power has given us everything we need for life and godliness through our knowledge of him who called us by his own glory and goodness. Through these he has given us his very great and precious promises, so that through them you may participate in the divine nature and escape the corruption in the world caused by evil desires" (1 Peter 1:3-4).

Peter was not the only one. The apostle John informs us that "everyone born of God overcomes the world. This is the victory that has overcome the world, even our faith" in Jesus Christ, God's Son (1 John 5:4,5). Jude, our Lord's half-brother, closes his brief epistle by proclaiming that Christ is able to keep us from falling and bring us into "His glorious presence without fault and with great joy . . ." (Jude 24). Paul insists that, in Christ, Christians everywhere "have been made complete . . ." (Colossians 2:10, NASB). And we must not forget our Lord's own direct promise: "If you remain in me and my words remain in you, ask whatever you wish, and it will be given you. This is my Father's glory, that you bear much fruit, showing yourselves to be my disciples" (John 15:7,8).

Are we not to believe, cherish and cling to all these verses? Have we misread them all these centuries? Have we expected too much from them?

No. They are to be taken at face value. Throughout history all believers have been of a like mind. Again and again, the church has demonstrated in blood its trust in these Scriptures.

The Reformation, the post-Reformation period, the Great Awakening of the 18th century, and the astounding missionary movements of the last two centuries found their calling and hope and power in the "great and precious promises of God." Gladly thousands went out and gave all to proclaim the forgiveness of God through the cross of Christ.

Is this history of trust in God and His Word merely a pilgrimage of ignorance, inadequacy and misplaced expectations? Has this been foolishness and an embarrassment for God? Can it be that for almost two thousand years God has left His people dangling and dancing in the wind?

Nowhere in Scripture are we told to regard these promises as less than dependable and complete. Nor are we ever told, "Yes, believe them, but in and of themselves they are inadequate." Nowhere are we told we need to look to the world system for additional "discovered" truths concerning God's sanctifying grace.

## Questioning the Integrity of God

When "Christian" psychology claims that victimization therapy is necessary, it also implies that Scripture is inadequate—a position that ultimately questions the integrity of God Himself.

I once preached a sermon that generally followed the outline of this book. Afterward, a retired gentleman, a man I know who longs to please God, came up and thanked me. Then he said with puzzlement in his voice, "One of our daughters once accused us of doing things to her that never happened." His is only one of many such stories I have collected over the past few months, stories of accusations of victimizations that never occurred, stories such as the following.

A foster father, who was a man of fine Christian reputation, was accused by a teen age girl, who had stayed in his home. She accused him of beating and sexually abusing her. He was immediately suspended from his job in law enforcement and an investigation was launched by the District Attorney's office. Under questioning, the girl admitted she had lied. She wanted to get even with the man and his wife because they would not let her stay with them. (They let her go because of her incorrigible attitude.) The investigation was immediately dropped and the man's suspension rescinded. Happy ending? Not entirely. A county social worker told him that even though the girl admitted lying, she (the social worker) still believed he was guilty.

## The Ubiquity of Victimization

More and more we live in a victim-obsessed social climate.[2] Parents and other adult family members are axiomatically considered guilty when charged with unloving behavior. Evidence is not needed. Victimization has become a given from which there is no escape.

Disturbingly, "Christian" psychology readily accepts and supports this view. Victimization has even infested the Christian community. Stories of neglect, abuse and mistreatment seem to be accepted at face value and are constantly discussed—even in church "care" groups. Even when such incidents are denied, it is insisted they must have occurred and must be shared.

How do we know that what is being related in the retelling of memories is true or accurate or complete? How do we know that what is being related is not imaginary—not just imaginary in the sense that one is making something up, but also in the sense that the person relating the information thinks it is true but it is not? Isn't it possible that an early childhood memory is nothing but a memory of the child's imagination? How do we know that one is not responding to the counselor's unspoken demands and pressures?

The following story illustrates this problem. A young seminary student was assigned, as a required part of his curriculum, to a small group whose basic purpose was to have each participant uncover and share some of the hurts and disappointments of his past. One day the group leader turned his focus upon this young man and his upbringing. The leader, experienced in this form of gentle "victimization" counseling, began asking him about his father.

The young man replied that his father was a wonderful man who had given him a solid moral foundation as well as an independence of spirit that had allowed him to resist peer pressure. His father had not only taught these values but lived them. The young man did express sadness, however, that his father was not a Christ-centered man and did not know the Scriptures. His father had once been active in the Lutheran church but had drifted away.

The group leader, sensing that here was an opening to help the young man realize his victimization, suggested that the young man must "really resent" his father because he had failed to provide his son with a true relationship with Christ.

No, replied the young man, he did not resent his father. He believed his father had done the best he could with the understanding he had.

The group leader was not satisfied. For several minutes he tried to get the young man to admit his disappointment and agree that his father had let him down spiritually. The young man refused to embrace this reasoning. He insisted again and again that though his father had not given him all he needed spiritually, he had given him all he was able to give. "I cannot resent him," the young man said, "because my father was not capable of giving me any more."

After several minutes of this impasse, the group leader moved on. But the young man sensed the leader's dissatisfaction and was aware that the leader believed he was holding back. The young man summarized his experience by writing that he could clearly see how such a methodology "can lead individuals to 'discover' hang-ups they don't have and cause ill will where none previously existed. The potential for evil is enormous."

Another story confirms this young man's insightful analysis. A youth pastor, married and with children, became sexually involved with a teen-age girl in his group. When the affair was exposed, the youth pastor publicly repented, asked forgiveness of the church, and resigned. But because a crime had been committed, he was arrested, tried and convicted. Counseling was required and the length of the sentence was partially determined by the psychologist's report. The youth pastor was in the psychologist's hands.

The youth pastor and his wife sought out the best Christian psychologists they could find, a husband and wife team, and attended all the sessions together. They expected scripturally-grounded counseling, but they soon learned that was not to be. Yes, Scripture was mixed in with a great deal of psychological terminology. And yes, each session did open with prayer, but right from the start the counseling centered on uncovering and working through the youth pastor's childhood. In addition, the counselors gave them a variety of books to read on such subjects as anger, guilt, and codependency, all written from a psychological point of view. At one time, the wife later said, it seemed as if she had been reading seven or eight such books simultaneously.

After a few sessions, the youth pastor and his wife asked if they might be counseled more directly from the Bible. Why, came the reply, hadn't they read the Bible? Why did they want to read it again and again? Did they do that with other books?

By this time, it was becoming obvious to the youth pastor and his wife that the counseling they were to receive wasn't going to be biblically centered. But because his family had been so torn by his sin and because of the impending prison term, the youth pastor laid aside his doubts and cooperated by accepting the direction the psychologists were leading. That direction was down the road of full-fledged victimization therapy. It was to be a devastating pilgrimage.

It began when the psychologists asked him to recall his first childhood memory. "Shame," he replied. He had lied to his father about a misplaced key. The psychologists immediately picked up on this opening. "Do you see what is in that?" they asked.

The youth pastor had to admit ignorance.

"You have displeased the (heavenly) Father," one of them replied, "and you are looking for a key to please him again."

This interpretation, the psychologist informed the youth pastor, was of God and for the youth pastor's benefit. With this "key" in hand, the psychologists began to unlock the youth pastor's "victimized" childhood. I put "victimized" in quotation marks because the youth pastor had deeply respected and admired his father. He loved him. (His father is now dead.) The youth pastor had always believed his father loved him and sought his good. His wife also believed this. Those who knew them well, relatives and friends, believed this as well.

But the psychologists disagreed. With each succeeding session, they dissected and reinterpreted the past from the vantage point of victimization. They showed the son that his father had not done the best he could have, that the father had been narcissistic, and that the father had used his son for his own self-centered reasons.

At one point, they told the youth pastor to remove his father's picture from the living room wall because it was an idol. (The church his father had pastored for many years had presented the picture to the youth pastor.) His removing the picture deeply offended his mother. At still another point, the counselors instructed him to obtain the family photo album and to look closely at all the childhood pictures of himself so that he might see how miserable he had been as a child. This action also alarmed his mother and caused her emotional distress. In fact, the therapy the youth pastor received caused a rift between his mother and him, as well as among other family members.

The psychologists' final conclusion for the youth pastor was this. You thought your dad was wonderful, but he wasn't wonderful at all. He victimized you rather than loved you.

For the wife there was this "comfort": the psychologists told her it wouldn't have mattered if her husband had had 50,000 wives, he was destined to commit adultery. Out of deep frustration and in total disillusionment with "Christian" psychology, the wife wrote, "It is such a pertinent question today: *whatever happened to the concept of sin?*"

Who can answer her question? Those who are engineering a Christianity built upon a view of reality that is essentially pathological? Where, O Lord, is your cross? Where are those who would be doubly cured of sin's damnation and dominion? Are there none anymore who will confess to being wretched sinners? Are there none who would willingly flee to the cross for pardon? Are there none who believe in its liberating and keeping power? Are none of us willing to sing:

> Alas! and did my savior bleed?
> And did my sovereign die?
> Would He devote that sacred Head
> For such a worm as I?
>
> Was it for crimes that I have done
> He groaned upon the tree?
> Amazing pity! grace unknown!
> And love beyond degree![3]

The whole process of victimization therapy is so subjective and arbitrary and manipulative that it begs criticism. What is amazing is how uncritically so many Christians have embraced this system as both Christian and scientific.

How can we help but question the scriptural validity of a process that encourages us to charge sins against another when the accused is unable to mount a defense? Proverbs 18:17 reminds us, "The first to present his case seems right, till another comes forward and questions him." Add to this the problem of past sins, already forgiven, now being resurrected, relived, and once again "unforgiven." Old hurts are rekindled, old bitternesses revived, and you have as unscriptural a process as could be imagined.

## The Monster of Codependency

Unfortunately, victimization counseling is not the only unscriptural tool in the toolbox of "Christian" psychology. Codependency is the latest hot item within evangelical circles. Its parameters are so broad and so loose that few can escape being accused. If allowed, it will subsume under its authority the scriptural teaching on Christian service and sacrifice.

Codependency is defined as the psychological "disease of those with a 'caretaker' mentality, who are over committed and over involved in the lives of needy individuals."[4] They "have a high need for keeping people dependent on them." The implications for the wife who is seeking to win her husband to Christ in obedience to 1 Peter 3:1-6 are serious. If he is labeled addictive, will she be found codependent? Will her gentle and quiet spirit and submissive demeanor cause her to be labeled an "enabler"?[5]

What causes someone to become a codependent? Can you say "low self-esteem"? Dr. Joyce Brothers, a well-known secular psychologist, puts it this way: "Co-dependency is a pattern of painful dependence on compulsive behaviors and on approval from others in an attempt to find safety, self-worth and identity."[6]

What are the characteristics of codependency? One Christian author who is considered a "resource person" on this subject lists over 200 features—and that, we are told, is not a complete list.[7] Of course, we must not allow ourselves to be overwhelmed by such numbers. Psychologists collect them. Minirth and Meier in their book *Happiness is a Choice* list 130 traits for what they call the "obsessive-compulsive" personality, 118 traits for the "hysterical" personality, 101 traits for "depressed" types, and 71 traits for a "cyclothymic" personality.[8]

Perhaps we could get things in perspective by viewing a small listing of codependency traits. All of them and any combination thereof makes us "it," and we are "it" whether we like it or not. This is the way the game is played and we don't have any say in the rules:

> [Codependents] are often passive-aggressive, lacking in trust, angry, rigid, controlled, and self-centered. Poor communicators, they may have problems developing intimacy in relationships and handling sexuality, and they often repress feelings and thoughts. Many are perfectionists who feel powerless, hopeless, withdrawn and isolated.[9]

One cannot help wondering, how many psychological "diseases" do such broad symptoms fit? Who among us can deny that at some time and in some situations we have not experienced some of those traits?

How many people suffer from codependency, you ask? Pick a number. But make it large—very large. One advertisement for a book on codependency by four Christian psychologists puts the number at approximately one in four Americans.[10] Some in the codependency field think one in four is much too low a number. Ninety plus percent would be a figure more to their liking. Their reasoning goes like this: anyone who has any relation with an "addictive" person is deemed to be codependent.[11] What this means for those who treat these unfortunates they do not say.

Pardon me, but who thinks up these things? Who decides what is "codependency" and establishes the criteria that determine the applicable standards? What presuppositions underlie the criteria? What scientific controls are applied to decide that 65 million Americans, or 100 million, or even 200 million are codependent?

They have us coming and going. On the one hand, for a sense of self-worth and meaning, I am told that I need to know others love me and value my contribution to their life. On the other hand, by seeking approval, security and worth, I can be accused of being codependent. What am I to do?

No wonder Scripture would appear to be inadequate to sanctify the believer. If what is taught concerning codependency is fact, it is a wonder that mankind, let alone the church, has made it this far. But I cannot believe that codependency is scientific. Codependency is conceptually subjective and structurally arbitrary, and it is counterproductive to a biblical understanding of self-denial.[12]

If codependency is to be taken seriously, how can any Christian have confidence in his walk with Christ? How could anyone escape being filled with anxiety or doubt over his or her service on Christ's behalf? How could any servants of Christ—be they teacher, missionary, preacher or rescue mission worker, filled with a zeal for Christ's glory and a compassion for the lost or poor or suffering, and giving and receiving much joy in their service—avoid an accusation of codependency? How could they defend themselves against a checklist of 200+ codependency traits?

## Was Paul Codependent?

Even the apostle Paul would have had a hard time avoiding the codependent label. Here was a man who practically demanded that the Corinthians love him as he loved them (2 Corinthians 6:11-13). He insisted he was their spiritual father in Christ and therefore they were to give preference to his teachings over any others (1 Corinthians 4:14-16). He told them to follow his example as he followed Christ's (1 Corinthians 11:1). He claimed he went hungry and sleepless in his worry over them (2 Corinthians 11:27) and that, if need be, he would gladly give all he had, himself included, for their benefit (2 Corinthians 12:15). If Paul were alive today, pastoring a church, would he not be branded an "expert at being codependent" and "addicted" to strength?

Certainly Christians may become over-extended—sometimes inadvertently, sometimes out of necessity because Christ calls them to it, sometimes sinfully to escape problems elsewhere, or sometimes because they sinfully enjoy the power that comes from people needing them. But let us call the sinful reasons sin rather than codependency. That's what they are.

God help us if we are going to start turning faithful, dedicated servants of Christ, who in their zeal may become overextended, into sick people diseased with codependency. Yet it will become unavoidable because the symptoms of this "disease" are so generic that it will be hard for many Christian psychologists to resist the temptation.

To whom shall we turn for guidance? Shall it be "Christian" psychology with its "X" number of steps to recovery? We shall surely see *Ichabod* written across the face of the evangelical church if we continue along these lines.

Enough is enough! It is time to get back to the Bible. It is time to put aside all our how-to, self-help books. It is time to abandon the "discovered" wisdom of psychotherapy and the support group mentality. Let us return to the Scriptures. Let us allow them to rebuke, correct, teach and encourage us into paths of righteousness and service with joy. For that is what God intended in giving them to us.

If, at the *Bema* seat of my Lord Jesus, He tells me I put too much confidence in Him and His Word and that I should have submitted to this new "discovered revelation," then to my shame I shall be "as one escaping through the flames." Yet, with all my heart I cannot imagine Him saying, "You trusted my Word too much."

## Spiritual Warfare

In the environment of "Christian" psychology and its victimization therapy and theories of codependency, the devil is free to play his game. Even if one is willing to incorporate the idea of satanic opposition, the way such "Christian" psychology functions in practice renders such a reality null and void. Satanic influence is rarely recognized as a direct cause.[13]

We might say that there is a humanistic, "horizontal" warfare evident in victimization therapy, but one would never know from this methodology the reality Paul describes so vividly in Ephesians 6:10-12:

> Finally, be strong in the Lord and his mighty power. Put on the full armor of God so that you can take your stand against the devil's schemes. For our struggle is not against flesh and blood, but against the powers of this dark world and against the spiritual forces of evil in heavenly realms.

How do these verses fit in with psychology's "victimization/low self-esteem is the cause of every sinful bondage" model of reality? How do you integrate them? "Christian" psychology can't and doesn't. How can so important a doctrine and essential element of reality be so ignored?

Did not Satan dog our Lord's footsteps from His baptism until the moment of His glory upon the cross—waiting for an opportune time to kill Him? Was Satan not at the crucifixion, urging us on in our frenzy of rage to crucify the Lord of Glory? Was he not among the crowd mocking and shouting, "If he is the Christ, let him come down now from the cross that we may see and believe" (cf. Mark 15:32)?

Was he not at Peter's side, there in the high priest's courtyard, dimly discernible by the light of the bonfire, sifting Peter like wheat, whispering in Peter's ear, "Deny Him. Don't be a fool. Save yourself. 'Skin for skin.' Look at him! It's all over. Don't be stupid." Was it not a satanic messenger who tormented Paul, hoping to discourage into sullen resentment and angry silence this great apostle of Jesus? As usual, however, he was only fulfilling God's plan to display to both Peter and Paul—and through them to us—the wonders of Jesus' love and the sufficiency of His grace.

Are not these incidents described in Scripture standard fare for us also? Was it only with an over-active imagination that Luther wrestled while hiding at Wartburg Castle, translating the New Testament into common German so that all might read God's Word for themselves? Legend has it that he hurled an inkpot at the devil for tempting him to quit. Good for Luther! We need more of that today. With wisdom born of combat, he wrote, "It is much easier to fight against the incarnate Devil—that is, against men—than against spiritual wickedness in heavenly places."[14]

Luther experienced what the biblical saints experienced (2 Corinthians 2:10,11), and his experience is not foreign to any believer who takes God's Word seriously. Each of us must daily wrestle with this evil and ancient foe. We had best have God's armor about us. Surely we ignore Satan to our own peril when we seek to tame sin with nonspiritual methods.

Scripture specifically warns us that believers can be caught in Satan's snare to do his will (2 Timothy 2:26), that he schemes to outwit us and will succeed if we are not watchful (2 Corinthians 2:11), and that he can masquerade as an angel of light (2 Corinthians 11:14,15). We also know he is constantly prowling around like a "roaring lion" seeking someone to devour (1 Peter 5:8). He is an enemy we must not ignore.

The great and fundamental weakness, the Achilles heel of "Christian" psychology, is its refusal to act upon the supremacy of the spiritual realm.[15] Our warfare may have physical, mental, and emotional aspects, but it is at heart a spiritual warfare, and we must fight accordingly (2 Corinthians 10:3-5).

"Christian" psychology is woefully inadequate for such a momentous task. It leaves us spiritually defenseless. A methodology of counseling that seeks the root of sinful behavior in pathological categories and its cure in an "appropriate" self-love, that ignores the cross and all that it signifies for the believer, will leave us dangerously unprepared for spiritual warfare when the day of evil comes. And come it will—and most ruthlessly on those who are least willing to acknowledge its reality.

Having just quoted Luther, I think it would be fitting to close this chapter by quoting the third stanza of his magnificent hymn, "A Mighty Fortress is our God." It expresses his own wartime experience and how he won the battle:

> And though this world, with devils filled,
> Should threaten to undo us,
> We will not fear, for God hath willed
> His truth to triumph through us.
>
> The prince of darkness grim—
> We tremble not for him;
> His rage we can endure,
> For lo, his doom is sure—
> One little word shall fell him.

What word is that, you ask? Not "what," but "Who." "Dost ask who that may be? Christ Jesus, it is He," sang Luther. "Christ and Christ only," John Bunyan declared.

Jesus is the way to victory. He is the way to life and holiness. He is the way, and no other.

---

## Notes

1    David Seamands, *Healing for Damaged Emotions* (Wheaton: Victor Books, 1981), p. 85.

2       We have so over used the term "victim" that we have trivialized its significance. Everyone and every incident in our life, no matter how minor, that can be interpreted as "negatively" affecting us, makes us a victim. Did your

mother publicly embarrass you for wetting your pants when you were four? You are a victim. The scar from that episode has probably significantly shaped your adult behavior and has contributed to your low self-esteem.

By making everyone a victim to one degree or another, we have made it more difficult to recognize and support true incidents of victimization.

3     Isaac Watts, "Alas! And Did My Savior Bleed?"

4     Jim and Phyllis Alsdurf, "The 'Generic Disease'," *Christianity Today* (December 9, 1988), p. 30.

5     Carol Travis, a feminist and a social psychologist, writing in the *Los Angeles Times*, makes a telling point along these lines when she says:

> Co-dependency theories therefore promulgate misplaced attributions of responsibility: Co-dependents learn that they are as much to blame for their spouses' problems as their spouses are, because they are "enablers." The partners themselves, however, are not considered responsible for their abusive, rotten or violent behavior, since, as one codependent writer says, they have a "progressive disease" and "can't help themselves" ("Just Another 'Disease' to Soothe Powerlessness," *Los Angeles Times*, March 5, 1990, p. B-13).

6     Joyce Brothers, "Getting Help for Co-dependency," *Los Angeles Times* (November 7, 1989), p. E-10.

7     Alsdurf, *op. cit.*, p. 30.

8     Frank B. Minirth and Paul D. Meier, *Happiness is a Choice* (Grand Rapids: Baker Book House, 1978), pp. 64, 89, 124, 205.

9    Alsdurf, *op. cit.*, p. 30.

In his Sunday column of March 4, 1990, Mark Lacter, Business Editor of the *Daily News* (a suburban Los Angeles newspaper), lists some of Melody Beattie's characteristics of codependency:

> [People] feel anxiety and pity when others have problems. They feel compelled to help someone solve a problem. They feel harried and pressured.

Lacter follows Beattie's words with these of his own. "If any of you haven't experienced these sensations from time to time, you're a rare breed."

Lacter's column is anything but friendly to codependency. He quotes child psychologist Robert Coles' comments printed in the *New York Times* that read: "I have a feeling we're soon going to have special groups for third cousins of excessive sherry drinkers." It is Coles' opinion, Lacter writes, that "the co-dependency movement has run amok and that it illustrates" (quoting Coles again) "how anything packaged as psychology in this culture seems to have an all too gullible audience" ("Helping Hand Might Have Tight Grip," *Daily News*, March 4, 1990, Business Section, p. 1).

10    Christian Book Distributors catalog (January-February 1990), p. 21. The advertisement is for the book *Love is a Choice: Recovery for Codependent Relationships*.

11    Alsdurf, *op. cit.*, p. 34.

12    Dr. Stan J. Katz, a secular psychologist, in his controversial new book, *The Codependency Conspiracy* (New York: Warner Books, Inc., 1991), makes the following charge:

> By creating so many different disease characteristics, the codependency leaders offer a slot for every-

one. We all must be codependent because we all fit at least one of the descriptions. This tactic is very good for book sales and lecture attendance. . . . But the tactic is also irresponsible. Most of the feelings and behavior listed as codependence traits are perfectly normal. They do not indicate that we came from dysfunctional families or are in one now. They do not prove we are addicts. . . . All they prove is that the authors of these lists have conceived a theory so broad, so multifaceted that it is virtually meaningless (pp. 16, 17).

13     When I speak of satanic influence, I am not speaking of it in the same way as those involved in deliverance ministries. I do not believe a Christian can be invaded or possessed by demons. Demon deliverance is simply the flip side of "Christian" psychology. Both advocate a truncated responsibility for sinful behavior. Both teach that other forces (i.e., "unconscious" or "demons") prevent the believer from being obedient to God and victorious in his life.

14  Roland Bainton, *Here I Stand: A Life of Martin Luther* (New York: Abingdon Press, 1950), p. 194.

15     I'm certain this charge will be vigorously denied. However, the very fact that "Christian" psychology approaches man pathologically, views and treats him as if he were basically a victim, claims that his major shortcoming is low self-esteem, refuses to acknowledge that a believer can truly come to maturity without victimization therapy—and the list could go on and on—all support my charge.

# 10

# By Faith—
# And Only by Faith

This chapter is about faith. Simple, unadulterated faith. Effective, here and now faith that loves Jesus and lays hold of the Word of God and never lets go or looks elsewhere. Such a faith has fallen on hard times. For it does not lead us to that school of thought that permeates "Christian" psychology.

In fact, it is not faith that "Christian" psychology promotes, but self-works. And, if it is self-works, then it distrusts faith and "works" against faith. If it works against faith, then it works also against Christ, who is ours by faith alone. If it works against Christ, then it also works against the power of Christ upon which our faith rests and which is perfected (that is, effectively experienced by the believer) when we are the most helpless. So then, if we pursue sanctification by human methods, is it true sanctification we obtain? Can God be pleased when our "faith" rests upon human means and human presuppositions?

## Faith and Pleasing God

We must always bear in mind that without faith, "it is impossible to please God" (Hebrews 11:6). The Christian life is nothing without a faith that permeates every aspect of our being and alters even the most mundane of our day-to-day thoughts and behavior. True biblical faith transforms the very nature of reality. We are now in Christ. Nothing is as it was. We work with new parameters of faith as we live out our new life in Christ. These parameters are not self-conceived but are taught to us by God Himself in His Word.

Chapters 11 and 12 of the epistle to the Hebrews clearly describe what we may expect from such a faith. Within these two chapters is pictured a faith that accepts and adjusts to God's perspective of this current age. This faith creates dissatisfaction with this world and a longing to see the city whose architect and builder is God. Happily such people bear the name "alien" and gladly uproot themselves to become pilgrims and strangers in the land of their birth. Such a faith takes captive their wills and opens their imaginations to holy possibilities. What was said of Moses is said of them: "He regarded disgrace for the sake of Christ as of greater value than the treasures of Egypt," and thus "he persevered because he saw him who was invisible" (Hebrews 11:26,27).

This faith makes Jesus Christ real, visible, immediate, powerful, our only hope and our only glory. It makes Christ more than savior. It allows us to claim we belong to Him and long for Him, and it fixes our eyes upon Him in order that we might imitate Him in a world that rejects Him and despises His cross. It moves us to concur with the words of Helen Roseveare who said, "I want people to be passionately in love with Jesus, so that nothing else counts."[1] It is this passionate love of Christ that is so often the missing ingredient in today's evangelical community.

Not too many years ago I put together a sermon titled, "Do You Know the Real Jesus?" I had become acutely aware that far too many Christians did not exhibit any genuine evidence that they knew the Lord. Every time I have preached that sermon the reaction has been astounding. I am always caught off-guard by the hunger so many express for a word that will encourage them to trust passionately in Christ.

Perhaps if the truth were confessed, Jesus Christ is simply not seen today as real and able to impact our lives with power. Words uttered by Alexander Maclaren a century ago are worth repeating. "The truth you do not live by becomes less and less real to you."[2]

## What's the Problem?

What has created this situation? Why does the faith of so many seem to lack the vitality of one who truly loves Christ more than life itself? We may offer a variety of reasons and pore over statistics until our minds are dulled, but one thing keeps coming to the fore. Ours is a third generation Christianity. Most of the young people in our churches have been reared and nurtured in a Christian environment, as were their parents. By and large most of them were saved at a very young age and have only known a Christian social setting. They have always been surrounded by things Christian. They are children of our own half-way covenant.[3]

The result is a people who often lack any real fear of sin, who often lack even a sense of personal sinfulness. Their commitment to Christ is anything but passionate. Of course, this is not entirely their own fault, for though they have been reared in a "Christian" setting, it is a setting that has been compromised by continual accommodation to the world. Neither they nor their parents have treated the sensuality of the prevailing secular culture as an enemy.

Evangelical Christianity is materialistic, consumeristic, entertainment-oriented, self-focused and self-indulgent. Intellectually, we are informed as much by the tenets of humanism as we are by the Scriptures. We are saturated with worldly values that have co-mingled with biblical ones. And while we defend our rights to indulge our freedoms, we are rapidly unraveling morally. Behaviors, dress and attitudes accepted today would have caused sincere shame a generation ago.

Let me illustrate. A young friend, saved in her late teens out of a wicked and destructive lifestyle, attended a Good Friday service with other young people in her age group. She was deeply moved by the message and the singing and by what the day meant to her. This was the day the Lord had taken upon Himself her sin and her punishment. As she was leaving the service, her mind was absorbed with the wonders of God's grace. She was therefore surprised and dismayed to find those around her immediately occupied with trite social conversation. Where should the group go and eat, what should it do for fun—the movies or miniature golf? She said it was as if no one had been in the service sixty seconds earlier considering the greatest moment in history.

Her story symbolizes for me a church that has become so compromised that it can go from the ridiculous to the sublime and back again and never be aware of the incongruity. Although we are heirs of Abraham's faith, we seem strangers to its dimensions and ramifications. An unquenchable passion for Christ and His glory, a desire to exalt Him in our bodies whether we live or die (Philippians 1:20), no longer anchors our day-to-day faith. Our faith seldom takes captive our wills or directs our desires.

The situation draws me back to C. S. Lewis' words: "For I am not sure, after all, whether one of the causes of our weak faith is not a secret wish that our faith should not be very strong."[4] If our Christianity isn't working, could it be because we don't want it to work?

We don't want our problems defined and resolved in the manner given us in the Scriptures, for to admit the answers are there would leave us very culpable indeed. We would be not just accountable for our actual behavior, but even more accountable for our efforts to mask our unbelief. We are unprepared for the way God may want to lead us. We have so over-emphasized the "unconditional-love" of God, so misused 1 John 1:9 with repetitious and empty apologies, that we neither count trials as "pure joy" (James 1:2) nor expect God to discipline us out of love or punish ("scourge," NASB) "every-one he accepts as a son" (Hebrews 12:6). This is the truth of the Christian's life of faith—a reality few seem willing to wel-come or accept.[5]

While we offer God a "behavior that works," He demands a faith that pleases Him. He demands that we believe in Hebrews 11 and 12 both passionately and joyfully. "Christian maturity is not only the result of growth," Alexander Maclaren once said, "it is the result of warfare. It is a race. It is mortifying the old nature."[6] It does not so much grow as we go as it must be deliberately built.

## Faith and Pain

Such a faith realizes that not only intense temptation but also affliction will be part of the believer's union with Christ. At times both temptation and affliction will come upon the believer. It will seem as if all the furies of hell are assaulting him and God is allowing it—and He is. A true faith in Christ understands Paul's words in Philippians 1:29: "For it has been granted to you on behalf of Christ not only to believe on him, but also to suffer for him."

The Puritan Richard Greenham once wrote:

> Whatsoever is upon you is from the Lord, and what-soever is from the Lord, to you it is in mercy; and whatsoever comes in mercy ought not to be grievous to you. What loss is it when the losing of earthly things is the gaining of spiritual things? All should be for your good, if you make your use of all.[7]

Hebrews 11 speaks of the jeers, floggings, imprisonments, death, destitution, persecution, mistreatment, homelessness and rejection that characterized those old Testament believ-ers who became heroes of our faith. Such trials, along with the personal testings of temptation and physical and/or emotional afflictions, have been and will continue to be real possibilities for anyone who has a faith that pleases God.

Faith in Christ is costly—and is meant to be so. If pursued, it will bring pain, disappointments and hurts, as well as moments of horrible personal failure. But even in the midst of these things, we need to listen to John Owen's sage advice to "take heed of spending time in complaints when vigorous actings of grace are your duty."[8] Sinclair Ferguson explains Owen's comment this way:

> The temptation of some is to be always discussing their problem and constantly looking for advice, instead of pressing on with the routine activities of their Christian life. This is not the scriptural way, which is to take the kingdom of God by force and press into it.[9]

It is here that "Christian" psychology does its greatest harm, for it functions only in an atmosphere of defeat, where one's faith is not "working" and where the believer is seeking to maintain peace both with and in sin.[10] "Christian" psychology did not bring on this sad state of affairs, of course; it is itself only a response to it. Yet it does exacerbate the situation with its pathological model of man as victim and its disdain for anyone who would dare to lay hold of the promises of God alone.

Hebrews 12:1 commands us to "throw off" both the sin and anything else that might hinder us and "run with perseverance the race marked out for us." We are commanded to "fix our eyes on Jesus, the author and perfecter of our faith" so that we "will not grow weary and lose heart" (Hebrews 12:2,3). These verses describe how the believer is to walk and why he is to do so. All who have endured and overcome affliction and temptation have done so in union with and through faith in the living Christ.

## Victimization as Anti-Faith

We are to accept affliction and temptation in simple trust. To fail to do so is to displease God greatly (Hebrews 10:38,39). That necessarily means the psychological concept of victimization cannot be realistic. The whole idea of the Christian-as-victim becomes unacceptable. If we believe God is sovereign, a Christian cannot be a victim (Romans 8: 28,29).

Indeed, to hold to such a view puts us at cross purposes with God's loving will for us in Christ Jesus. Do we think we shall share in His holiness without affliction and suffering or dying to self? Do we think God is satisfied with partial loyalty or partial holiness or a casual love? Is it through indifference or deliberate intent that we have failed to remember that our God is a jealous God?

Without question we shall experience pain, hurt and disappointment—but we are not to understand these things as the world does (2 Corinthians 5:16). That which the believer suffers is not the pain of victimization, but the pain of pruning done by the Father (John 15:1-4). We are not to view it as the wound of betrayal, but the wound of love. "He punishes everyone he accepts as a son." If we are sons, we cannot be victims; we cannot consider our pain the pain of betrayal. Though others may intend to do us evil, yet God intends their evil actions to do us good—that we shall reap a harvest of righteousness and peace (Hebrews 12:11).

As believers, we must by faith understand that all that happened to us before we were redeemed was to prepare us to flee to the cross for forgiveness of our sins through faith in Christ. Do we think it was by accident we heard the good news—and believed it? As one who is now in Christ, by faith I understand that all things work together for my good—**all** things. Not for my earthly pleasure, or my earthly happiness, or my comfort or security, or anything else to do with my life on this earth. By faith, even the worst of circumstances are subdued and made expressions of God's grace.

## Passionate Love for God

What is good for me above all else in this earthly sojourn is that I might long for God, love Him above all else, yearn with all my being to glorify Him and visibly demonstrate His sustaining grace as I pursue Him. God alone knows what is required to bring this about. Mine is to be the faith that knows without a doubt that God will do this and must do this if I am to please Him.

Helen Roseveare spoke to this issue when she wrote:

> Jesus said, deny yourself, take up your cross, and follow me. Where was he going? To Calvary. Paul wrote, "I have been crucified with Christ." Somewhere, we've gone off course. We've got to be willing to say, what matters is not what I'm worth, or what people think of me, but that people come to know and love Jesus.[11]

The point of following Christ is not entertainment, or fun, or even a means to wholeness as the world understands these things. Crucifixion is violent and deadly. There seems to be little glory in it. Yet there is no glory short of it. If God disciplines us, we are to bring the pain of it to Him and give it to Him so that we might be comforted and strengthened in our faith. In that way we, like Abraham, can give "glory to God."

If it is God inflicting the discipline, we can count it all joy. Not as the world counts joy, but as Christ counts joy. Listen to what He said in the garden:

> As the Father has loved me, so I have loved you. Now remain in my love. If you obey my commands, you will remain in my love, just as I have obeyed my Father's commands and remain in his love. I have told you this so that my joy may be in you and that your joy may be complete. (John 15:9-11).

That is strange talk for one about to suffer death by crucifixion. Yet the author of Hebrews tells us, "For the joy set before him, [Jesus] endured the cross, scorning its shame" (Hebrews 12:2).

Without the faith described in Hebrews eleven and twelve, Christianity is little more than shadow boxing. There will be no violent warfare with sin, no pressing on toward God's high calling in Christ, no real conviction that it is even worth the effort. Why? Because Christ's joy is absent from our hearts.

God values our faith too much to spare us the rigors of whatever will strengthen it. "Those whom I love, I rebuke and discipline" (Revelation 3:19). Our Lord despises a half-hearted faith (Revelation 3:16) that demands and takes but never wants to be tested. Peter wrote to some believers that their faith was being put to the test so that it "may be proved genuine and may result in praise, glory and honor when Jesus Christ is revealed" (1 Peter 1:7). This is the end purpose of our calling in Christ.

Yet this testing should not leave us considering ourselves victims as if God had turned on us. It is given to make Him who is invisible more dear and our joy in His reality the richest outpouring of our love. The rewards of faith are not just coming by and by. They are also immediate and powerful in the securing of our perseverance.

Andrew Murray once wrote, "Do not think that it is a little thing and easy, to live the life of faith. If we are the heirs of Abraham's faith, then the Father makes great demands on our faith." He demands that we trust Him explicitly. So much so that when God asks it of us, we will, like Abraham, be able "without any promise, in fact in apparent conflict with all the promises, to obey God's will to the very uttermost."[12]

## The God of the Patriarchs

For Abraham and Isaac, God was Jahweh-jireh, the God who provides (great deliverance).[13] When Abraham raised the knife, when Isaac lay helplessly bound beneath the poised blade, both were absolutely dependent on God. There was nothing they could do to "help" God. Either God was sufficient or they were mad. Either He was Jahweh-jireh or He was Jahweh the bizarre, Jahweh the bloody, Jahweh the lunatic. But He was and is Jahweh-jireh. One cannot help thinking that both Abraham and Isaac left Mount Moriah with an even greater faith in the sufficiency of God to meet their needs, whatever they might be.

That was then. However, this is almost the 21st century. Charles Wesley could write, "O for a thousand tongues to sing, my great redeemer's praise, the glories of my God and King, the triumphs of His grace!" That was then, but this is today. Surely our praise rings hollow for a Christ we hold to be insufficient. It is not from Scripture, of course, we draw such a conclusion, but from our "ravaged" fortunes. The fault is not with our faith, we insist, but with our past. We are but victims of its unrelenting demands.

Indeed, the time is long past when we should have been questioning ourselves. Is there not something faithless in saying that what Christ does not require, we must—that is, visit and muse painfully aloud over each "imprisoning" outrage once visited upon our defenseless psyches. Are we not faithless, as Scripture measures faith, when we say the children of the cross are "destined" to be held captive by mocking phantoms, who, as fluttering harpies snatch from them their Master's grace? Enough! It is not the insights of "Christian" psychology we need to hear, but the Lord speaking to us from His Word. It is no true faith that is void of victory and joy and confidence and obedience in the living Christ!

Do we want to be heirs of a half-way covenant and a limited God?

## The Road Back

How are we to find our way back home? The answer of the Scripture is, "By faith." By faith we are to receive the promise of the Spirit, by faith we live by the Spirit, and by faith we "keep in step with the Spirit" (Galatians 3:14 and 5:25). The Spirit intends that our faith "might not rest on men's wisdom, but on God's power" (1 Corinthians 2:5).

"And without faith it is impossible to please God." We must come back to this. We must come back to the absolute sufficiency of this. It is the only foundation upon which all else can be built: "Faith expressing itself through love" (Galatians 5:6), faith that leads to obedience (Romans 1:5), and faith that not only receives Christ, but is "rooted and built up in him" (Colossians 2:6,7).

Faith was meant to perturb, Luther said. Faith is meant to stir us up and turn our world upside down. Such a faith cannot be created and experienced by a tradition tainted by humanistic presuppositions. It must come from God, and He gives it only to the heart that hungers and cries out for the substance of things not seen. It is only given to the heart that cries out, "I want to know Christ and the power of his resurrection and the fellowship of sharing in his sufferings. . ." (Philippians 3:10). He only gives it to the heart that strives to love much because it has been forgiven much and is amazed and overwhelmed that such could be possible (Luke 7:36-50).

God wants to give us such a faith (Ephesians 3:16,17). God wants to take our weak faith and make it strong, mature and fruitful. He wants us to prove Him. He wants us to possess the faith of Abraham to which Paul referred in Romans 4:20 and 21:

> Yet he did not waver through unbelief regarding the promise of God, but was strengthened in his faith and gave glory to God, being fully persuaded that God had power to do what he had promised.

What an awesome statement. "God had power to do." This is what faith lays hold of. As we focus on Christ, realizing our own inability to be like Him, and cry out to God, broken and humbled and hungry for the reality of our new life in Christ, then and only then will God strengthen our faith and prove His power to us. "But we have this treasure in jars of clay," Paul wrote, "to show that this all-surpassing power is from God and not from us" (2 Corinthians 4:7).

From God, not us. That's faith.

---

## Notes

1    Helen Roseveare, "The Cost of Loving Jesus," *Christianity Today* (May 12, 1989), p. 45.

2    Leslie R. Keylock, "Alexander Maclaren," *Fundamentalist Journal* (January 1989), p. 58.

3    The Half-Way Covenant was an attempt by the early Massachusetts Puritans to resolve the dilemma of how to include the children of their own sons and daughters, many of whom could not give evidence of a conversion experience, within the covenant community.

By speaking of this "third-generation" of evangelicals being children of our own half-way covenant, I am referring to how the evangelical community tries to bring its children into the covenant community of God's visible elect. Instead of practicing infant baptism, we practice child evangelism. In a way, we reverse the puritan approach. We lead the child to an acceptance of Christ at as early an age as possible and then baptize them. Having thus secured for them a place in the kingdom of heaven, we try to nurture them in a completely "Christian" environment—church programs, camps, schools and anything else we think will protect them from the world.

However, as with the Puritan half-way covenant so it is with ours. The results are less and less satisfactory. If you doubt this, talk with the youth pastor of any fair sized youth group. The level of personal sin and accommodation to worldly values is high and deeply corrosive.

I am convinced that this is a key reason "Christian" psychology is so popular. We are looking for some method to rescue an increasingly spiritually impoverished covenant community. But because the methodology we are so fervently embracing is not derived and structured from the Word of God, the very way we seek to rejuvenate ourselves only reflects and reinforces the problem we say we want to solve.

4   C. S. Lewis, *Christian Reflections* (Walter Hooper, ed. Grand Rapids: William. B. Eerdmans Publishing Co., 1967), p. 43.

5      A recent incident highlights this. A believing woman called into a Christian radio psychiatrist to relate how her 12-year-old daughter had leukemia. It had been brought into remission but now it had flared up again, and this time required much more extensive and painful treatment. Her daughter often was in great pain and so discouraged that she wanted to die. It was all the mother could do to keep her daughter going.

The situation had made the mother very angry with God. She didn't say over the radio what she had said or done, but she admitted that afterwards she had felt guilty for her behavior.

The psychiatrist hurriedly assured the woman she had done nothing wrong. God loved her and didn't hold her behavior against her. God understood her feelings and knew she had to express them the way she did. At no time was she lovingly reminded that, yes, she did need to repent because she had sinned.

God does not accept being "raked over the coals" by one of his redeemed people. It is not OK to get angry with God and "vent" our ill feelings and criticisms in His face and then say we have done no wrong.

One can honestly sympathize with the woman's pain and frustration at watching her daughter suffer. Many have been in similar situations and have been tempted to rage and accuse God of meanness. But she should have been told that it was right for her to feel guilty about her behavior. In getting angry with God she had sinned. In all gentleness, she should have been encouraged to repent and told why.

By telling her that she had done nothing wrong, the counselors not only misrepresented God, but also robbed the woman of an opportunity to glorify God. By repenting, she would have acknowledged that God is good and loving toward all of his people, including her and her daughter. She would have admitted that he is righteous and just in all he does, that he is sovereign over everything and every aspect of her life, and that he is bringing her to maturity and holiness through this painful hardship.

6    Keylock, *op. cit.*, p. 56.

7    *The Golden Treasury of Puritan Quotations*, compiled by I. D. E. Thomas (Chicago: Moody Press, 1975), p. 13.

8    Sinclair B. Ferguson, *John Owen on the Christian Life* (Edinburgh: The Banner of Truth Trust, 1987), p. 111.

9    *Ibid.*

Owen admonished people who were inclined to dwell on their problems, "Get up, watch, pray, fast, meditate, offer violence to your lusts and corruptions; fear not, startle not at their crying or importunities to be spared; press on to the throne of grace by prayers, supplications, importunities, restless request. This is the way to take the kingdom of heaven. These things are not peace, they are not assurance; but they are part of the means that God hath appointed for the attainment of them."

10    Joseph Alleine wrote, "Cursed is that peace which is maintained in a way of sin. Two sorts of peace are more to be dreaded than all the troubles in the world; peace with sin, peace in sin" (*An Alarm to Unconverted Sinners*, p. 64).

[11] Roseveare, *op. cit.*, p. 45.

[12] Andrew Murray, *The Secret of the Faith Life* (Fort Washington: Christian Literature Crusade, 1957), p. 5.

[13] Nathan J. Stone, *The Names of God in the Old Testament* (Chicago: Moody Press, 1944), p. 51.

Stone has this to say about Abraham and Isaac's relationship:

> Surely out of this experience of Jehovah's delivering grace there must have come a purer, more spiritual relationship of love between this father and son. This must have been one lesson the experience was intended to convey.

# 11

# Describing
# the Man of Faith

"And without faith it is impossible to please God" says the writer of Hebrews (11:6). The context of this verse makes it clear that it is impossible to say God is pleased with a faith that never moves beyond the "just let Jesus into your heart" stage of Christianity, which is puzzled by the expression, "Lord Jesus," and that never reflects any deep and on-going relationship with the living and all-powerful Christ.

So what characterizes a person of pleasing faith? What distinguishes him or her from others who say they believe? What traits do they exhibit that convince others that here is a man or woman who truly believes?

I believe there are seven such traits. No one holds these traits perfectly, but they are being perfected by the Holy Spirit as we respond to Christ's command, "Follow me!"

## Thankfulness

No matter how many ways I put together my list, the one at the top is always thankfulness. I cannot imagine anyone truly believing in Christ who does not have a lifestyle of thankfulness toward God, a deep, overwhelming, constant, pervasive sense of gratitude.

Thankfulness for what? First of all, for one's salvation. Would once a day be too often to recall Paul's memorable words, "What a wretched man I am! Who will rescue me from this body of death? Thanks be to God—through Jesus Christ our Lord" (Romans 7:24,25)? We have been "rescued." And the words "what a wretched man I am" have become for us "what a wretched man I was."

Thankfulness also comes from the knowledge that God, who "did not spare His own Son" for our benefit, will graciously continue to provide us with whatever we need to live the victorious Christian life (Romans 8:31,32). Have we become so familiar with these words that they no longer amaze us? I wonder if our growing concentration on our hurts and disappointments makes it more difficult for us to be honestly humbled by God's grace?

We are to be thankful for God's sovereign direction in our lives. "Give thanks in all circumstances," Paul wrote, "for this is God's will for you in Christ Jesus" (1 Thessalonians 5:18). That includes even the tears God's grace will bring us. When affliction befalls us or temptation besets us, is there truly a welling up of gratitude within our hearts for God's merciful hand upon us? Can we say, "It was good for me to be afflicted so that I might learn your decrees" (Psalm 119:71)?

Can we accept the death of a child, a devastating illness, loss of worldly comfort and security, or even love, as the will of God for us in Christ Jesus? Can we accept them with thanksgiving as stripes of discipline, expressions of afflicting mercy, and necessary wounds that conform us to the image of His dear Son? Must we not first conform to Christ as crucified before we can be conformed to Him as glorified?

## Dependence

Second on my list is a trusting, confident, absolute dependence on Christ. We ought to consider anew what Christ meant when He said: "I tell you the truth, unless you change and become like little children, you will never enter the kingdom of heaven. Therefore, whoever humbles himself like this child is the greatest in the kingdom of heaven" (Matthew 18:3,4).

Too often we relegate the idea of childlike trust to our salvation "faith" experience. Let us instead relate it to John 15:5 ("apart from me you can do nothing"). Little children can do nothing apart from their parents—nor do they plan on doing so. The dependence of a child is a life of unthought-out expectation. He expects his parents to feed, love, protect, comfort, play, teach, discipline, guide and generally be there for him. He cannot imagine his parents in any other context. He confidently and expectantly believes in his parents' faithfulness.

So it is to be with us. We are to believe expectantly in God's faithfulness. We are to be confident that God has the "power to do what He promised," and that He will use that power on our behalf. We should naturally expect nothing else or nothing less. We are His children. Too often, we allow ourselves to be drawn away from this day-to-day necessity by the self-sufficiency of our culture. In addition, our culture, which has so worked into our churches, works deliberately against our developing any concrete expressions of true dependence on Christ. Whether in asking for our bread or asking for victory over sin, our culture offers a counterfeit for that which God longs to provide.[1]

## Holy Fear

Third, one who truly believes exhibits holy fear. This trait may make us nervous, for we have become used to basking in God's "unconditional love" (i.e., undemanding love). But notice what the author of Hebrews tells us:

> [Noah,] when warned about things not yet seen, in holy fear built an ark to save his family. By his faith he condemned the world and became heir of

the righteousness that comes by faith (Hebrews 11:7).

It should be a sobering and even frightening thought that our faith in Christ is an open declaration of God's judgment upon this world. (Also see Philippians 1:27,28.) How diligent we ought to be that unbelieving men find our faith credible!

"In holy fear" Noah obeyed God. One commentator wrote this about Noah's response to God:

> On the one hand he expressed deep reverence to God, and on the other hand he was terrified because of the coming destruction. He was filled with holy fear at the prospect of God's judgment on the sinful world. For if he had not believed God's warning, he would not have been afraid. . . . Noah's faith stood diametrically opposed to the unbelief of the world.[2]

The unbelieving world does not fear God, but we ought to. We walk through a perishing world. The cross unequivocally declares this. Out of a holy fear of God we flee to Christ in order that we, too, might be saved from the coming wrath. Noah, in holy fear, preached God's coming wrath for 120 years. His warning came not by words alone, but also by his faithful construction of the ark—day in and day out. By faith we, too, are to be building our Christian life day in and day out, warning men by our reverent actions about the inevitable and sure consequences of their sin.

A holy fear of God is an essential element of one who possesses a true faith in Christ. At our own peril we forget that God is a jealous God who chastises His erring children. We cannot casually hide behind John 1:9 and think that all is well.

Would any of us be willing to accept that a lack of "holy fear" of a majestic and holy, sovereign God might bring "pain and disappointment" into our lives? It did for the Corinthians, whose lack of respect for the Lord's table brought sickness and even death (1 Corinthians 11:27-32). In the real world God will not be mocked. If one chooses to please the sinful nature, one will "reap destruction"—Christians included (Galatians 6:7,8).

Does God still operate this way toward His people? Easy believism, easy repentance, and now our acute awareness of our victimization all tend to make us think God is willing to be restrained about honoring His holy name. But there is no true faith devoid of a holy fear that moves us to obedience.

## Perseverance

Fourth, let us add the word *perseverance*. "But he who stands firm to the end will be saved," our Lord said to His disciples (Matthew 10:22). There is no faith that does not persevere. The recipients of the epistle of Hebrews were warned, "You need to persevere so that when you have done the will of God, you will receive what he promised" (Hebrews 10:36).

Faith is living out (doing) the will of God. We have no idea what that may entail. There are no promises that it will come easily or painlessly. Paul reminded the young churches of Galatia that "we must go through many hardships to enter the kingdom of God" (Acts 14:22). The recipients of Peter's first epistle had suffered "grief in all kinds of trials" (1 Peter 1:6). The clear message is that believers ought to expect trouble, hardship and difficulties. We shall not be excused from the hard realities of our calling, which is a call to war.

Since New Testament times we who are in Christ have been subject to difficulties and persecutions. At times, horrible and terrible circumstances have dogged our way. Some have come upon us because we obviously bear the name of Jesus. Others make no sense, search as we may, and God does not give us the light we think we need to understand. But we walk by faith and witness always to the grace of God in Christ.

We live within a world order that is in rebellion against God and under the dominion of the evil one. Wretched things happen in such a place. We must take the world's hostility against God seriously. The world would much rather live with its miseries and horrors than yield to and worship the living and true God. Through it all, God commands us to persevere to the end and reminds us that if we shrink back, our faith will not be pleasing to Him (Hebrews 10:38). We are to endure hardship as necessary discipline.

Far too often, however, we resent and resist any interference on God's part that might deprive us of our deepest desires. Many Christians who sing, "It is well with my soul," are lying. It is not well with their souls because they are not persevering, and they have no intention of doing so, because they are bitter and hostile toward God and mourn over their "victimization" at His hands. Others are little better, for they "persevere" with a cold, stony, stoic demeanor that constantly reminds God how much they are doing for Him despite His lack of reciprocity.

But that is not perseverance. Biblical perseverance comes with a modifier. Not only are we to persevere through the most wretched of circumstances if God so requires, but we are to do so with joy! Almost invariably in Scripture, trial and joy go together. We are to rejoice that we share in the sufferings of Christ (1 Peter 4:12-14). James tells us to count it "pure joy . . . whenever you face trials of many kinds" (James 1:2). Paul reminded the Thessalonians to "rejoice always" and "give thanks in all circumstances" (1 Thessalonians 1:16,18). Habakkuk, looking at the suffering and devastation facing Israel, wrote:

> Though the fig tree does not bud and there are no grapes on the vines, though the olive crop fails and the fields produce no food, though there are no sheep in the pen and no cattle in the stalls, yet I will rejoice in the Lord, I will be joyful in God my Savior (Habakkuk 3:17,18).

Joy in our life in Christ is always expressed in proportion to how well we see and love "Him who is invisible" and how much we really want to see "the city with foundations, whose architect and builder is God" (Hebrews 11:10). Our supreme example is Jesus, "Who for the joy set before him endured the cross, scorning [despising, NASB] its shame" (Hebrews 12:2). What was that joy? John Piper thinks, "His joy is in *our* redemption which redounds to *God's* glory."[3] So joy anticipated became joy experienced.

Piper believes that when Jesus rose from His knees at Gethsemane, "there flowed through His soul a glorious sense of triumph over the night's temptation." Piper goes on to say:

> I think there was joy in Gethsemane as Jesus was led away—not fun, not sensual pleasure, not laughter, in fact not anything that this world can offer. *But there was a good feeling deep in Jesus' heart that his action was pleasing to his Father, and that the reward to come would outweigh all the pain.* This profoundly good feeling is the joy that enabled Jesus to do for us what he did.[4] (Emphasis his.)

What provokes our joy as we persevere? Is it not proving our God before a cynical and wicked world? Is it not showing that He is with us in our every trial and that He is sufficient? Is it not in experiencing His power, His grace, His very presence—and by thus proving Him—that we bring Him glory and ourselves joy? Have you never risen from your knees triumphant over all that would destroy your faith? Is there no joy in the Lord at such a moment—a joy that remains to strengthen us to faithfully persevere in Jesus' name?

Helen Roseveare was a missionary doctor for twenty years in what is now known as Zaire. In 1964 there was a rebellion in which Roseveare was taken captive and held for five months. During these months she was beaten, abused and raped. After her release she went home for two years, then returned to Zaire to continue her medical mission work for another seven years. She is a woman of immense courage in Christ, a woman completely sold out to Christ.

Is there joy in being so at the disposal of Jesus? Do you suppose were I to ask her, "Was there joy inexpressible and glorious in serving Jesus those twenty years in Zaire despite the terrible suffering," that she would say, "Yes"? I do. But let us allow her to speak for herself:

> I'm a fanatic, if you like, but only because I believe so strongly that nothing counts except knowing your sins have been forgiven by the blood of Jesus. We've only got this short life to get others to know the same truth.[5]

We seriously need to ponder Roseveare's words. We need to realize that only those who truly grasp what it means to be "forgiven by the blood of Jesus" will want to and can persevere to the end with "joy inexpressible and full of glory."

## Victory

Let us allow the apostle John to introduce the fifth trait of those possessing biblical faith:

> This is love for God: to obey his commands. And his commands are not burdensome, for everyone born of God overcomes the world. This is the victory that overcomes the world, even our faith. Who is it that overcomes the world? Only he who believes that Jesus is the Son of God (1 John 5:3-5).

Our faith in Christ, flowing from our love of God, is the means by which our Lord gives us victory over sin, temptation, discouragement, momentary defeat, hard circumstances or whatever else we can think of.

Faith gives us the victory in two ways. First, faith puts us in contact with the resurrected Son of God Himself, the Lord of Glory who has all authority and power in heaven and on earth. He puts His power to work for us to insure our victory

(2 Corinthians 12:7-10). Second, faith changes our attitude concerning the things of God. His commands no longer seem stifling and intolerable—nor unreasonable. Faith allows God's grace to empower me to say "no" to sin and "yes" to righteousness and godliness (Titus 2:11,12).

Certainly it is true that sanctification is a process that continues from the moment of one's regeneration until the moment one stands in the Lord's presence. But Scripture never hints that there could be little or no discernible progress after a few years, or even a few months, of union with Christ. One who believes in Jesus Christ is expected increasingly to show victory over sin and Satan. The idea that our "unconscious mind" can block the work of the Holy Spirit simply denies one of the most clearly taught promises concerning my life in Christ—namely, victory over temptation and the power of sin. Let it suffice to say that without faith it is impossible to please God, and God the Holy Spirit clearly says that faith, and faith alone, in Christ is the means by which we overcome the world system with its temptations and afflictions.

## Reality of Christ

The sixth trait is this: Jesus Christ is delightfully real to one who possess a faith pleasing to God (Psalm 37:4 and 1 Peter 1:8). True faith produces a distinct hunger to experience His living presence, and faith partially satisfies that hunger. Faith places us in a living fellowship with Christ. It convinces me that He is for me right now and exercising His power on my behalf right now, strengthening my faith as needed right now that I might glorify Him right now in my present circumstances. This does not mean a giddy, be happy, don't worry life. It means that, by the grace of God, I understand the ramifications of what it means to be in Christ and willingly, with increasing joy, embrace them.

I do not persevere for the sake of a life under control. I persevere because my Lord Jesus lives! Whatever this present generation understands faith to be, if it doesn't acknowledge the reality of our Lord's living presence—right now, right here, dominating my reality—it is not a faith that pleases God. If the immediate presence of the living Jesus is not characteristic of our faith, then the scriptural claim that God will provide an escape from whatever temptation we face will only be so much empty rhetoric possessing no convincing authority. The fleshly moans of sinful pleasure will eventually be far more persuasive. Evidently this is what is happening with an ever increasing number of professing believers.

## Longing

The seventh and final trait of those who wholeheartedly trust in Jesus is longing—longing to actually see our Lord. Love will never be faithful if there is no longing. The apostle Paul, as he faced his martyrdom, wrote:

> I have fought the good fight, I have finished the race, I have kept the faith. Now there is in store for me the crown of righteousness, which the Lord, the righteous judge, will award to me on that day—not only to me, but also to all who have **longed** for his appearing (2 Timothy 4:7,8; emphasis added).

Should not there be in a believer's heart a desire to obey Him, share Him, and experience His grace in the moment by moment living out of one's Christian testimony, as well as a passionate longing to see Him? Sadly, despite all the talk and writing about the Tribulation and Jesus' Second Coming, there appears to be little genuine longing to see Him.

C. S. Lewis once commented, "After all, we do not usually think much about the next world till our hopes in this one have been pretty well flattened out . . . ."[6] Living in America is easy and pleasurable and entertaining, with much to enjoy and possess. With so many sensual experiences at our fingertips, the need for Christ's company often seems secondary and even tertiary. In fact, some of us appear downright reluctant to give up the riches of this life for something as abstract as "eternal glory." Death and suffering, deprivation and sacrifice—things that once made eternity immanent and imposing—seem distant and almost unreal in our day. Hence a lack of any sincere longing for Jesus. We are hesitant to wrestle with the implications of Hebrews 12:1, which tells us to "throw off everything that hinders and the sin that so easily entangles, and . . . run with perseverance the race marked out for us."

Oh, we do not deny Him or His coming. We are simply in no great hurry for Him. Such a position leaves us as idolaters clinging to the temporary pleasures of this life. Do we really think that if Jesus comes back before we have experienced some of the earthly pleasures we so intensely covet, we shall spend eternity regretting that we missed out on them?

If we will not long for our Savior, we will not truly follow Him. Certainly there will be little of the cross and eternity in our Christianity.

## How Do We Obtain the Seven Traits?

An overwhelming thankfulness, a confident dependence, a holy fear, perseverance with joy, a life of victory, a personal awareness of the living Christ, and an unquenchable longing for Jesus—all these are characteristics of a true believer whose faith is pleasing to God. We cannot attain them by our own efforts. We cannot make ourselves lovingly follow God. We can only cry out to God to give us a believing heart for His great name's sake. And God is willing to deepen and strengthen our faith if we will come to Him as we ought.

How is that, you ask? Listen: "This is the one I esteem: he who is humble and contrite in spirit, and trembles at my word" (Isaiah 66:2).

Do we really know in whom we believe? Will we put aside our own wisdom and contrivances and methodologies to improve upon the "deficiencies" of "just trusting in Jesus," and cast ourselves once more upon the sufficiencies of our God? The author of Hebrews wrote:

> Therefore, since we are receiving a kingdom that cannot be shaken, let us be thankful, and so worship God acceptably with reverence and awe, for our "God is a consuming fire" (Hebrews 12:28,29).

Do we want such a faith, or will we continue to build our own solutions? We can construct our own version of Christianity and still have hearts that are ice-cold toward the real Jesus, yielding nothing to Him but self-satisfying words that commit us to nothing—neither faithfulness, nor purity, nor an undivided and passionate love, nor glory. Yet all these things are rightfully Christ's, joyfully rendered by us to Him.

------

## Notes

1.     There recently appeared in the bulletin of a nearby local church an announcement inviting members to attend a "Christians in Recovery" conference. The announcement declared that over 90% of Americans come from "dysfunctional homes—that is, homes that are not just damaged by, say, alcoholism or drugs, but also by such disorders" as workaholism, perfectionism, depression, compulsive behavior, intimacy problems, etc. These problems, we are informed, affect the family as much as does alcoholism. The announcement continued with these words:

> For years millions of Americans have had to struggle alone with these kinds of dysfunctions. But times are changing and many of these individuals, including Christians, are tearing down the "walls of denials" and opening doors of opportunity for emotional and spiritual healing.

The announcement then described the conference as a chance for healing and making us more aware of dysfunctional families. The keynote speaker was to address the topics of the 12-step method of recovery and "Facing Codependency as a Christian." Workshops on such subjects as shame, sexual addictions, eating disorders and a host of other subjects were to be offered.

The announcement strongly implied that we are all sick, coming as we do from "sick" families, and we all need help in "recovering from our sicknesses." We could easily change a word or two and pass out the same announcement at the Elks club. No one, it seems, comes from a home where the children are sinners as well as the parents.

When I read such things as this and realize what is taking place at the local church level, I find myself almost frantically asking myself, "What has Jesus Christ and his Word to do with my life?" Evidently, for an ever increasing number of believers, the answer is, "Very little."

2    Simon J. Kistemaker, *Hebrews* (Grand Rapids: Baker Book House, 1984), pp. 318, 319.

3    John Piper, *Desiring God* (Portland: Multnomah Press, 1986), p. 108.

4    *Ibid.*, p. 109.

5    Helen Roseveare, "The Cost of Loving Jesus," *Christianity Today* (May 12, 1989), p. 45.

6    C. S. Lewis, *Christian Reflections*, Walter Hooper, ed. (Grand Rapids: Wm. B. Eerdmans Publishing Co., 1967), p. 37.

# 12

# The Mystery
# of His Power

It is fitting that we follow our discussion of faith with one
on God's power. In Scripture, faith and grace go hand in
hand. You can't have one without the other. Also, when we
speak of the grace of God, we are at the same time speaking
of His power.

At times, the words are almost interchangeable. We are
saved by grace, yet Paul called the Gospel of grace "the power
of God for the salvation for *every one who believes*" (Romans
1:16). Our Lord Himself showed the wonderful interrelated-
ness of these two words when He said to Paul, "My grace is
sufficient for you, for my power is made perfect in weakness"
(2 Corinthians 12:9). The Holy Spirit gave us more mind-bog-
gling hope when He led Peter to write, "His divine power has
given us everything we need for life and godliness through
our knowledge of him who called us by his own glory and
goodness" (2 Peter 1:3).

Surely such verses were given to encourage believers by
giving them something concrete and dynamic to lay hold of in
time of necessity. Yet "Christian" psychology, by its presuppositions, challenges the reality of these promises. Is it justified

in doing so? If it is, how are we to understand these verses? Just what is meant by the "power" of God?

From the first page until this one, the key concept underlying everything in this book has been the outworking of God's power—visible means versus invisible workings, methodology versus mystery. How is the power of God realized or effectually experienced in the believer's day to day walk in and with Christ?

Power instinctively fascinates us all. It is unavoidable in making life "work." Without the authority and power to accomplish a goal—whether the task is mundane or global in scope—nothing will get accomplished. Power is the great passion of all mankind. Whatever passions may drive men to do what they do, the passion to wield power underlies them all. Our fall into sin wove this dark thread into the very fabric of our depraved psyche and made it a dominating characteristic of our sinful humanity. Devoid of true submission to Christ, all of us will corruptly use power.

We are constantly tempted to scheme how to acquire power and exercise it for our own advantage. We don't have to be taught this passion to bring others under our control; the youngest child among us relishes the despot's role. Ambitious individuals have bent every bit of wit and cunning, sacrificed their families, compromised their integrity, ruined others, shed rivers of blood and devoted vast treasures, time and energy in order to grasp the scepter of unchecked power.

Let us admit, however, that such men and women are no worse than the rest of us. If we do not compete with them and out of envy wish their ruin,[1] then we cheer them on and mimic them in our own petty fashion. In our fleshly minds, nothing so approaches the divine as the exercise of power.

## Like Father, Like Son

Satan's great envy of God became man's great envy of God. Man longs to have the power to impose his will in whatever way he chooses, when he chooses, upon whom he chooses. Where once he exercised power as a servant of creation for the glory of his Creator, now he does so as an envy-bloated lord rebelling against his rightful sovereign. In Eden, man wielded power in humility and love, assured of God's love. Now he wields power arbitrarily, carnally, coercively, often brutally and always self-centeredly.

Ray Bradbury, the famous science fiction writer, spoke for all post-Edenic men when he was interviewed on radio about the Voyager space craft's historic fly-by of the planet Jupiter. He said, "Man was kicked out of the Garden of Eden, now he is going back." Few times in history has man spoken with such candor.

Even as believers we find the temptation almost irresistible to substitute works for faith. Unless we understand the enormous proclivity of the flesh to seek power, we will not be alert to how easily we can misunderstand, doubt and seek to substitute our own ideas and methods for God's power.

Since earliest church times Christians have sought to use man's methods to achieve what they believed to be God's ends. The history of the church is haunted by the debris of ambitious and/or zealous "believers" who have sought to improve Christianity for God's sake and in Christ's name. Despite the scriptural warnings that our weapons of war are not those of this world (2 Corinthians 10:3,4), and despite our Lord's admonition that we can do nothing apart from abiding in Him (John 15:5), believers continue to build their faith and God's church upon wood, hay and straw. The appearance is often deceptively imposing and persuasive, but the end result is that our faith comes to rest on man's wisdom and not God's power. The edifices we build are misleading and carnal. Thus they are without eternal significance.

## Power Through Powerlessness

The great sorrow is that we are not aware of how much we have maligned God or tried to steal his glory. Yet, when we study the Scriptures, we cannot help realizing that for man truly to know God and be accepted in Christ and experience the reality of God's power through faith in Christ, he must gladly relinquish all ambitions for worldly power. He must be willing to be powerless and without self-glory before his fellow man and the One who alone is almighty. He must become as Jesus was before men—helpless and defenseless. Consider the response of the apostle Paul when the Lord informed him that his weakness exalted Christ's power:

> Therefore I will boast all the more gladly about my weaknesses, so that Christ's power may rest on me. That is why for Christ's sake, I delight in weaknesses, in insults, in hardships, in persecutions, in difficulties. For when I am weak then I am strong (2 Corinthians 12:9b,10).[2]

How many of us truly rest upon our Savior in such confident helplessness? If we did, "Christian" psychology would have few advocates and even fewer dependents. Please note that Paul didn't receive relief from trying circumstances. No, the tormentor remained. Temptations still crept about in the corners of his mind, waiting to imprison his will. Yet he received something much more valuable than relief. Christ's power rested on him! The reality of God's power strengthened him to persevere with joy. From that point on, Paul almost relished the conflict, especially when it appeared that the deck was stacked against him.

Note the types of conflicts Paul mentions—weaknesses, insults, hardships, persecutions and difficulties—five terms that fairly cover the spectrum of conflict a believer might encounter in living out his life in Christ. Surely included in this list are those things that psychologists tell us ought to cause dysfunctions, hurts, disappointments, addictions, victimization consciousness and low self-esteem.

So, on what does Paul depend to overcome these problems? Methods incorporating psychotherapy and emotional catharsis in a group setting? No! Rather, he depends on Christ's power (grace). And whom does Paul seek out for strength and victory? To his small group and its 12-step methods? To a therapist who will lead him through his victimization? No! Rather, he turns directly to the Lord Jesus who is the power and wisdom of God.

This does not negate the church or its necessary role in the believer's maturity and encouragement. The church is still the place where he is to minister to others the grace God has given him.[3]

But each believer is to have a growing, dynamic, personal relationship with the living Christ, whose power flows directly into his life. Thus the foundation and stability of his victory over the world, the flesh and the devil is in Jesus Christ. It is not in a greater appreciation of his self-worth, or in a small group identified with a particular sin, or in a psychologist using methodologies dependent on human power and derived from human wisdom.

The issue is this: Are we glorifying God in our obedience and humility? Is Christ exalted in our responses? Is it truly His grace that is sufficient (1 Peter 1:6,7)? If this is not our goal, then we have not helped anyone, though we may put a leash on our sin, tame our behavior, and feel good about ourselves again.

## God's Power in the Age of Grace

The verses quoted earlier (2 Corinthians 12:9,10) also reveal something of the mystery of how God's power works in this age of grace. Indeed, there is a mystery to God's power that befuddles the carnal mind. It cannot comprehend a power that does not make one more important, or at the very least protect one from personal harm and humiliation. The understanding of God's power is hidden behind the cross from carnal eyes. Was ever God's power exhibited more openly than at the cross? Was ever His glory more obvious than at the cross? Yet, who recognized this on that fateful day when men ridiculed the One who was making possible their salvation?

Even in His earthly ministry, even before His great mani-
festation of power at the cross, Christ displayed the mystery
of the power of God in stunning and salvatory ways, which
puzzled, confused, angered and challenged those who thought
power meant self-glory and who thought God was very much
like themselves (Psalm 50:21). If we would understand, even
in part, the working of the power of God, then we must consider the earthly work of Him who even now contradicts our
"need" for significance and glory.

## Power in the Life of Jesus

When we consider the earthly ministry of Jesus, we are
made aware of a strange phenomenon. The one who speaks
for God, who wields God's power in a unique and disturbing
way, is a nondescript laborer, not a lord; an itinerant teacher,
not a philosopher-king. He has no compelling form or
majesty. No influential men surround Him, no wise counselors advise Him, and those closest to Him are uncertain,
self-centered, greedy and cowardly. He envies no man's
throne and the one He had He joyfully yielded for the greater
welfare of His subjects.

Still, the power that flows from this man is like none anyone has ever seen. It fascinates us and compels our attention.
It does what no earthly power has ever done. It is compassionate, perfect, effective, unmistakably divine and desperately needed. Yet no one is coerced by it; no one is forced to
bow down. Only those who believe truly experience and benefit from His power. He does not use or manipulate the weak
and dispossessed. Nor does He seek His own glory, but rather
the glory of another.

He says His burden is light and His yoke easy. Those
weighed down by the unceasing demands of this world's
power-lords find rest under His authority. He demands no
tribute ("If you love me," He said), yet He never ceases to
give. Jesus Christ, the meek and lowly one, came preaching
the kingdom of God, performing signs and wonders and dis-

playing a form of power that no man had ever possessed. It made envious those in seats of authority, those who lorded it over others. Had they possessed such power, the world would have been theirs for the taking—and they would have taken it.

Yet no armies assembled themselves on His behalf. Crowns were not offered. Conquests were not proclaimed. Banners were not waved. Nations were not subdued, nor any people enslaved. He who came to seek and serve the lost, who came to offer His life a ransom for many, had no need for the trappings of power that men so cherish. A cross was a more fitting and lasting emblem of His glory, and far more powerful for the setting up of an eternal and righteous kingdom. What better way for ridiculing the forces of darkness?

Jesus Christ, the meek and lowly servant, walked among the people of Galilee and Judea, displaying the authority of God in words and acts of unparalleled compassion. He introduced new meaning for the word *power*. The paralytic walked, the demons fled, the dead lived, the blind saw, and thousands were fed with a simple word of thanks. He needed only to speak and it was so. Yet never was a bruised reed broken or a flickering wick extinguished. Those touched by His power rejoiced and danced and followed Him.

His is the power that seeks out the corrupt of heart and purifies them. It reaches down into the forgotten places where the disinherited are crowded and probes the lost shadows where the damned are imprisoned. He sets them free. He breaks the power of their sin. He raises their heads to the light and makes them sons and daughters of God. His is a power that denies the long-cherished belief that if God works His power in this world, He must do so through men and their means, or He does not work at all. Yet Jesus did the work of God independent of every cherished power structure. He still does.

He asked no man's permission to give sight to the blind or to raise the dead. He forgave the sinner and ignored the methods and standards of men. He freely dispensed God's grace and in the process set the teeth of the establishment on edge. His power was, is, and always will be a power that glorifies God. Such a man embarrassingly humbles the powerlords of this perishing age, exposing their ignorance, contradicting their arrogance, and making them resentful. For His is a power that gives too much, asks too much, changes too much. It is too alien to our understanding of the purposes of power. It does not glorify us so we reject it and reject Jesus. "It is of Satan," we said. "It is against Caesar," we said. "Crucify Him," we said. But for those who believe, Jesus Christ is "the power of God and the wisdom of God" (1 Corinthians 1:24).

## The Key to Power

This is the key—believing God. "This is my Son, whom I have chosen; listen to him" (Luke 9:35). Faced with a power they could not explain, comprehend, subdue, corrupt or bend to their own purposes, faced with a power that was too costly to believe in, the lords of this age crucified the Lord of Glory—and their subjects applauded. They still do. The coercive power of man seemed greater than the serving power of God; self-serving power appeared greater than sacrificial power.

After all, He who could save others from death would not or could not save Himself. He who proclaimed the coming kingdom of God with signs and wonders had none for Himself. He who alone is the only true king of all the earth was overcome by petty, jealous despots who dealt with Him in the most degrading way possible. Where was His power? Why was He hiding it? Surely this is not glory. His own followers, those who had experienced firsthand His power, who had believed His teachings, who had seen His glory—even these denied Him, scattering into the night of betrayal, deserting the power of eternity, fleeing before the taunts and threats of mortal rulers.

How, then, can we speak of the awesome greatness of the power of God? What does it mean? How does it work? When do we see it or experience it? Is it only so many religious words and self-induced emotions?

## The Mystery of God's Power

There is a mystery here. Men dare God to display His power, to compare it to theirs. He lets them boast and mock. He humbles Himself. The sea will not part nor will fire fall from heaven. (Someday it will, but not now, not yet.) Jesus will not ask for the assistance of 72,000 angels who burn with holy indignation at the blasphemy of arrogant men. Instead, He asks the Father to forgive His tormentors—and we do not understand the power of His words.

Thus to the unbelieving eye, to the man without the Spirit, the power of man seems greater, more obvious, more immediate, more effective, more glorious, more desirable than the power of God in a crucified, powerless Jesus.

Oh, if only fire might fall from heaven, then we would believe! But our demand is ignored. God does nothing. There is only silence (except for the echoing words, "It is finished"). We look for a sign, but there is nothing to see (except the shadow of the cross). So it seems to the eyes and ears of unbelieving hearts. Their ears cannot hear the shouts of victory— "He lives!" They cannot see the resurrected One because they will not go to the foot of the cross. Only from that vantage point can one see the living Jesus.

In their pride, they do not "seek him; in all [their] thoughts there is no room for God" (Psalm 10:4). "Man the measure of all things" fills their minds. What he cannot rationalize remains chaos, what he cannot rule he destroys, and what will not exalt him he rejects. The fool says in his heart there is no God, no necessity of the cross, no resurrection of Christ or of you and me, no love of God in Christ, no new life in Christ, no power in Christ. Pity the fool. Pity the world ruled by such fools.

Weep and fear for the church when it stops believing in these things, when it no longer has the faith to distinguish between earthly power and heavenly power.

Only as we deeply think on these things will we thoroughly grasp, in the very marrow of our bones, the chronic resistance, the innate hostility, the deep-seated unwillingness of man to believe in God's power in Christ or to submit to God's condition for experiencing that power. In Christ, God openly offered His power to resolve all of man's difficulties, failures and conflicts. And through the cross man openly rejected that power.

Therefore God has hidden the expressions and experience of His power in the very cross men rejected. His power is only evident to, and effective in, the lives of those who are willing to believe in God's "foolishness," who are willing to be contrite and meek and lowly before the cross and their neighbors, who are willing to let go of all envy and worldly power. Only those willing to become nobodies and fools in the world's eyes will understand and live by the power of God in Christ.

Such people are the "foolish things of the world" God has selected to "shame the wise," and "the weak things of the world God chose to shame the strong" (1 Corinthians 1:27).

## The Power of the Cross

When one considers all the thousands fed, all the sick and diseased made well, all the crippled healed, all the demons banished and even all the dead raised—all these together cannot compare to the awesome display of God's power at the cross hidden beneath the guise of death.

The cross is the true and perfect revelation of God's power for those who are willing to flee to Christ and be crucified with Him to the world. In response, our fleeing becomes the true and perfect expression of our faith, the foundation upon which Paul's words in 2 Corinthians 12:7-10 rest and are given integrity.

The power of God creates a new person in Christ. A former enemy is a dear friend. A worthless servant is now a faithful son or daughter. Who outside Christ can see God's power in all of this?

Oh, the wonderful sufficiency of the power hidden in the message of the cross—who can really comprehend it? None of us, I think, but millions of us have experienced it. Jesus Christ, exalted in our weaknesses, glorified in our difficulties, magnified in our hardships. Nothing needs to be added to this power. Nothing human clings to this power. Nothing human belongs to this power. Nothing human limits this power or assists it or manipulates it. Nothing human is like this power. God has seen to that.

"For the message of the cross is foolishness to those who are perishing," who hold fast to the illusion of personal autonomy and power. The very moment men think something needs to be added to the cross, at that moment it ceases to be a cross that divinely saves and provides the sure foundation for our sanctification. Even our faith, at that moment, ceases to rest on God's power.

In and of itself, the power of the cross meets the deepest yearnings of our hearts and the deepest needs of our being—spiritual realities that can only be spiritually understood (1 Corinthians 2:10-16). Though they are invisible realities, they are still the very essence of life. Though the world refuses to acknowledge the evidence of God's power, those who have been truly saved know it to be real. Their personalities change, their behavior changes, their attitudes change, and their goals change. All these have changed because their basic motives and their understanding of reality have changed:

> . . . for Christ's love compels us, because we are convinced that one died for all, and therefore all died. And he died for all, that those who live should no longer live for themselves but for him who died for them and was raised again (2 Corinthians 5:14,15).

This is at the heart of all the believer does and thinks and says. And it will become visibly evident both to himself and the world around him.

By faith in the power of the Lord of the cross, we become citizens of a country we have only read about. We trust and love a resurrected Savior-King we have never seen. We also rejoice for His sake in a way of life that puts us at odds with the world around us—even sometimes to our harm.

Daily we demonstrate in our lives the death and resurrection of Christ. We proclaim by word and deed the new man or woman in Christ in a body that is outwardly perishing. The world cannot believe in such truths. We who are in Christ can only grasp them in part, yet benefit from them daily—what we cannot always articulate, we live. It is the power of God alone that makes this possible, for "we have this treasure in jars of clay to show that this all surpassing power is from God and not from us" (2 Corinthians 4:7).

## The Dimensions of God's Power

All of this brings us to consider again the Holy Spirit's great revelation in 2 Corinthians 12:7-10, a revelation meant to let the believer understand the dimensions of God's grace as well as what our faith ought to anticipate. Standing behind these verses and giving them authority is the life, death and resurrection of our Lord Jesus. These verses openly and inarguably declare that, under the most difficult and stressful of circumstances, the power of Jesus Christ is immediately and constantly available, effectively working to give the believer victory. This direct and personal intervention of Christ gave Paul the assurance to say he is "glad" when he faced insults, weaknesses, difficulties, and whatever else would drag him down.

Perhaps this is why Paul could so adamantly say that with the temptation God "will also provide a way out so that you can stand up under it" (1 Corinthians 10:13). Granted, I have a part to do (Philippians 2:12, Ephesians 6:13), but even this has been made possible by God making me a new creation in Christ and using His power on my behalf (2 Corinthians 5:17; 1 Corinthians 15:10; Colossians 1:11,29).

It is God's power that makes it possible for me to fulfill the ministry He has given me (2 Corinthians 3:4,5 and 4:7), to be transformed into the Lord's likeness (2 Corinthians 3:18), overcome the devil (Ephesians 6:10-12), endure extreme hardship with great patience and joy (2 Corinthians 12:7-10), and resist the temptations of sin (1 Corinthians 10:13). "Christ in you the hope of glory," Paul wrote to the Colossians, and surely these verses offer us no small guarantee that the "kingdom of God is not a matter of talk but of power" (1 Corinthians 4:20).

Taken together, these verses contradict "Christian" psychology. God says there is no temptation I cannot resist with His help. My Lord Jesus says His grace is sufficient to carry me through my trials. Is God guilty of hyperbole? Am I guilty of a thoughtless and naive literalism? Or are the practitioners of "Christian" psychology guilty of contradicting the Spirit?

When we say we believe in the message of the cross, yet proclaim that the power of sin has not been broken and cannot be broken until all the "bad conditioning" we have received is uncovered and purged, are we not denying the reality of the working of God's power in the cross (Ephesians 2:8,9)? Sanctification consists of the Holy Spirit applying God's power to protect, deliver and mature the believer. It is a supernatural working (Galatians 3:3). We pursue and cooperate in the working out of our salvation, but when all is said and done, our sanctification is by the power of God working with and within a yielded and dependent Christian. The mature believer is identified by the fruit of the Spirit, not by a "behavior that works."

Even unbelieving men can develop methodologies that change behavior or help them work through their emotions or put a leash on destructive habits. This is what present-day psychology is all about. But in light of verses such as those above, it is not enough for the Christian to simply change his behavior or get in touch with good feelings or gain control over his sinful compulsions. Even more important is how that change is effected. We would do well to give thoughtful consideration to these words by John Owen:

> Mortification from a self-strength, carried on by ways of self-invention, unto the end of a self-righteousness, is the soul and substance of all false religion in the world.[4]

Only the Christian changes, resists, endures and rejoices because the power of Jesus Christ is at his or her behest. This is what points to the supernatural; this is what exalts his Lord. This is what man can not duplicate but only feebly and pretentiously try to imitate. Only the Christian can show off God's greatness by his total dependence on the power of Christ to give victory in his weaknesses, hardships, difficulties and persecutions. Through His power, God gives us the victory, we demonstrate His reality, and He is glorified.

Spurgeon, preaching on Psalm 50:15 ("And call upon me in the day of trouble; I will deliver thee, and thou shalt glorify me," KJV), stated it this way:

> God and praying man take shares. . . . First here is your share: "Call upon me in the day of trouble." Secondly, here is God's share: "I will deliver thee." Again, you take a share—for you shall be delivered. And then again it is the Lord's turn— "thou shalt glorify me." Here is a compact, a covenant that God enters into with you who pray to him, and whom he helps. He says, "You shall have the deliverance, but I must have the glory."[5]

God desires that we have more than a life in which we are under control. He wants us to know Him and delight in Him and love Him from the heart. He wants us to declare with integrity that through faith in Christ there is genuine forgiveness of sin and newness of life—life lived in supernatural power that allows us to overcome enemies both supernatural and fleshly.

No matter how unintentional it may be, the evangelical community is being taught not to look to the Word of God for understanding and solving its problems, not to experience the reality of God's power promised to us in Christ and by Christ, but, rather, to depend upon the word of the psychologist to live a victorious Christian life. Christ said, "My grace is sufficient." "Christian," psychology says, "not without my assistance."

Scripture emphatically insists we fix our eyes upon Jesus. It is emphatic in telling us to forget what is behind. Scripture instructs us to focus on Christ to appreciate fully what it means to be new creations in Christ Jesus, to live for new goals and new purposes (Ephesians 4:20-24), and to function with a new source of power, which comes directly from Christ and which energizes our wills to a new and godly obedience.

The past is not to be allowed to obstruct or limit our present pursuit of Christ. Whatever went on in our lives before Christ was lived on a different level for different reasons and was energized by a different power. But if Christ is our ambition, if Christ is our great purpose in life, then His grace will be more than sufficient in our moments of weakness, hardship, persecutions, insults or difficulties. Remember, Paul considered his satanic tormentor an obstacle to his Christian life; Christ considered it a necessity.

If we are not experiencing the reality of Christ's power, we need to check out our faith from the foundation up, not start devising human answers to explain away our failures or construct methodologies to achieve the righteousness we think grace failed to provide. To those who say they cannot obey God, try as they might and pray as they might, let us seek the resolution to their failure in Scripture and before the cross, not in man's tools invented to assist the Holy Spirit.

## Confidence Is No Guarantee

The Galatian heretics were confident they were using godly means to insure their acceptance by God; so, too, were the Colossian heretics. Paul condemned both. He pointed out that neither one was based on the promise of God in the sufficiency of Christ as taught in the Scriptures and confirmed by the Spirit.

"Christian" psychology finds itself in the same predicament today. It, too, stumbles over the wonder of God's grace and the great mystery of His power.

In 1 Corinthians 1:17, Paul writes that Christ sent him to preach the Gospel without the "wise and persuasive words" of men, "lest the cross of Christ be emptied of its power." Jesus Christ and Him crucified was a demonstration of God's power that "made foolish the wisdom of the world" so that no one could say God needed his help. Even our faith is to rest exclusively on God's power, not on any insightfulness on our part. This is why Paul was so sharp toward the Galatians when he scolded them, "Are you so foolish? After beginning with the Spirit, are you now trying to attain your goal by human effort?" (Galatians 3:3).

Perhaps we ought to ask ourselves the same question. Are we? If the popularity and influence of "Christian" psychology is any indication, then I fear more than ever the answer is "yes."

Let us take care that we do not find ourselves envying and resisting the power of God with man-made imitations. Those who love and choose such vain substitutes consider the message of the cross mere foolishness; thus they perish in unbelief. "But to us who are being saved," Paul wrote, "it is the power of God!"

It is the power of God, both then **and** now.

## Notes

1      This reminds me, of a line from Shakespeare. Speaking of Cassius, Caesar says, "Such men as he be never at heart's ease./Whiles they behold a greater than themselves/And therefore they are very dangerous." (William Shakespeare, *The Complete Shakespeare*, Alfred Harbage, ed. Baltimore: Penguin Books, 1969, p. 902.)

2      One cannot help comparing Paul's attitude, both about extreme problems and overcoming them, with "Christian" psychology's broad assertion that past hurts and sins are responsible for our present inability to say "no" to sin.

3      That believers are to help one another and bear with one another is a New Testament given. Christianity is not a "rugged individualism" affair. Biblical counseling by godly men and women has always been a part of God's means of grace. Believers can struggle with sin, and accountability to another believer and God's Word has helped many to victory. But even here, the Holy Spirit is the energizing, effectual power (Ephesians 3:20).

4      Sinclair B. Ferguson, *John Owen on the Christian Life* (Edinburgh: The Banner of Truth Trust, 1987), p. 145.

5      Charles Spurgeon, quoted by John Piper in his book, *Desiring God* (Portland: Multnomah Press, 1986), p. 134.

# Epilogue

We have reached the end, but not of our controversy. I fear it is just beginning. I fear a great struggle looms ahead for all of us. The outcome is in doubt.

When I began this book, I mentioned that I was perturbed, fearful, alarmed and angry over what Christian psychologists are doing. Now that I have put my objections down in order, I must admit that my antipathy and opposition are more deeply embedded than when I began.

I don't know what was anticipated when Christians started "integrating" psychology and Scripture; but whatever the purpose, we have created a threat to the integrity of Christ and His Word that will surely undo us if it continues.

What I find even more disturbing is that I am not sure we want to acknowledge how bad the situation has become. The impression that so many people are apparently being "helped" seems reason enough to avoid the issue. Perhaps, also, the evangelical community has come to reflect the view of society as a whole—that science can solve every problem, including social and personal ones. As our faith in the reality of Christ has weakened and become more of a cultural expression of an inherited spirituality, so too, we have seen a corresponding rise of faith in psychology.

What is puzzling and even incongruous about all of this is that despite the increasing influence and popularity of anything labeled "psychology" (and the proliferation of counseling centers and clinics that "non-judgmentally" treat every conceivable addiction, disease and dysfunction), one does not see our society becoming more gracious or moral. It seems to be unraveling with increasing speed.

Rape, abortion, abuse, mistreatment, immorality, depression, family collapse, suicide, venereal disease, lack of integrity, deliberate mismanagement for purposes of greed, drug use and personal violence all seem to be multiplying. And all our self-help, group-help, and professional help combined do not seem able to reverse this flood. We have become a people who define ourselves as "victim-driven dysfunctionals addicted to diseased behavior."

How pathetic compared to the biblical perspective of man! Yet evangelicals seem determined not to be left out. More and more we are defining ourselves pathologically and becoming obsessed with our personal happiness. We are becoming increasingly intimate with psychology—albeit with a Christian label—believing it presents a better and more immediate hope for achieving happiness than does the Scripture. Evangelicals have become captivated with psychology, assured that it cures problems of the heart that Scripture never even addresses, and that it does so with more effectiveness, compassion and understanding than does the Bible.

A massive contradiction is developing in our churches, that has gone largely unnoticed. A contradiction between what is being preached and taught from the Word of God and what is being preached and taught by "Christian" psychology.

On Sunday, I listen to the Word of God being preached that speaks of sin and righteousness and judgment, of grace and the power of God. On Monday, I attend a seminar that tells me my failure to obey God is not due to a carnal attitude but to my victimization by my family. Alas, that has made me a dysfunctional person seeking a proper self-esteem through "wrong choices."

Do we really believe there is no contradiction between the two? Where are we being led? Do we even know? Wherever it is, I will no longer follow. The poet Robert Frost once wrote:

> Two roads diverged in a wood, and I—
> I took the one less traveled by,
> And that has made all the difference.[1]

Taking the road less traveled by—that imagery captures very well those who commit themselves to live and die, victoriously and joyfully, by the words Christ gave them. Today, it is not an overly crowded road. Certainly it is narrow. And difficult at times. Yes, we mustn't hide that fact. But for everyone who takes that road, the grace of Christ walks with him, sustaining the weary pilgrim with unlimited and unconquerable strength. In addition, it is a road that runs straight toward that city "with foundations, whose architect and builder is God." Christian, therefore, has no fear of losing his way. The same cannot be said of those who have married themselves to the words of "Christian" psychology.

I know in this age it is risky to take an adamant stand against attempts to integrate psychology with Scripture. But I must, for integration has led us into this wasteland.

So what ought we to do? Surely it is obvious. The church ought to get rid of "Christian" psychology. The church ought to call those who are married to it to repent and come back to a true belief in, and submission to, the Scriptures as the only sure guide and counselor for the believer. "Discovered truth," so called, must no longer subordinate the clear revelation of God's truth. The wonder of God's grace—not works—must be preached.

Christ and Christ only—not men—must be exalted. For in Him and only in Him "are hidden all the treasures of wisdom and knowledge" (Colossians 2:3) The church must believe this, preach this, teach this and live this. Anything less dishonors our Lord. Anything less helps no one. But more and more it seems, this is the road less traveled by, and between "ought to" and "will" there is often this vast wasteland that only the most courageous will cross.

Times, they are indeed changing. Pathological man has entered the church, showing us the wounds of his victimization, denying culpability, displaying the ragged and dirty garments of his self-worth, soliciting our sympathy, demanding that we preach Christ and Him crucified in non-judgmental phrases, in more self-esteeming terms.

Is this not a different gospel? Are we ready for the consequences it shall bring upon us all?

---

## Notes

1   Robert Frost, "The Road Not Taken," *Complete Works of Robert Frost* (New York: Henry Holt and Company, 1949), p. 131.

If you would like more information about the intrusion of psychological counseling theories and therapies into the church, please write to:

PsychoHeresy Awareness Ministries
4137 Primavera Road
Santa Barbara, CA 93110

# OTHER BOOKS FROM EASTGATE

***PsychoHeresy: The Psychological Seduction of Christianity*** by Martin and Deidre Bobgan exposes the fallacies and failures of psychological counseling theories and therapies for one purpose: to call the Church back to curing souls by means of the Word of God and the work of the Holy Spirit rather than by man-made means and opinions. Besides revealing the anti-Christian biases, internal contradictions, and documented failures of secular psychotherapy, PsychoHeresy examines various amalgamations of secular psychologies with Christianity and explodes firmly entrenched myths that undergird those unholy unions.

***Prophets of PsychoHeresy I*** by Martin and Deidre Bobgan is a sequel to *PsychoHeresy*. It is a more detailed critique of the writings of four individuals who attempt to integrate psychological counseling theories and therapies with the Bible: Dr. Gary Collins, Dr. Lawrence Crabb, Jr., Dr. Paul Meier, and Dr. Frank Minirth. The book deals with issues, not personalities. For some readers, this book will be a confirmation of their suspicions. For others it will be an encouragement to be steadfast in the faith. For still others it will be a difficult challenge. Yet others will simply take a stronger stand for integration and all it implies.

***Prophets of PsychoHeresy II*** by Martin and Deidre Bobgan is a critique of Dr. James C. Dobson's teachings on psychology and self-esteem. In addition, several chapters are devoted to a discussion on self-esteem from the perspective of the Bible, research, and historical development. The book evaluates teachings rather than personalities. The purpose of the book is to alert readers to the inherent spiritual dangers of psychological theories and therapies and to uphold the sufficiency of God's provisions through Jesus Christ, the Holy Spirit, and the Word of God for all matters of life and conduct.

# MORE BOOKS FROM EASTGATE

*The Grand Demonstration: A Biblical Study of the So-Called Problem of Evil* by Dr. Jay E. Adams penetrates deeply into the scriptural teaching about the nature of God and the existence of evil. Nearly every Christian asks this question: "Why is there sin, rape, disease, war, pain, and death in a good God's world?" But he rarely receives a satisfactory answer. Nevertheless God has spoken clearly on this issue. Moving into territory others fear to tread, Dr. Adams maintains that a fearless acceptance of biblical truth solves the so-called problem of evil.

*Four Temperaments, Astrology & Personality Testing* by Martin and Deidre Bobgan answers such questions as: Do the four temperaments give true insight into people? Are there any biblically or scientifically established temperament or personality types? Are personality inventories and tests valid ways of finding out about people? How are the four temperaments, astrology, and personality testing connected? Personality types and tests are examined from a biblical, historical, and research basis.

*12 Steps to Destruction: Codependency/Recovery Heresies* by Martin and Deidre Bobgan provides essential information for Christians about codependency/recovery teachings, Alcoholics Anonymous, Twelve-Step groups, and addiction treatment programs. They are examined from a biblical, historical, and research perspective. The book urges believers to trust in the sufficiency of Christ and the Word of God instead of the Twelve Steps and codependency/recovery theories and therapies.

*Lord of the Dance* is a spiritual growth book for women. Deidre draws unique parallels between the training of a ballet dancer and a disciplined, graceful walk with God: from the love of dance to the all-consuming love for Jesus; from the need for correct body placement to the need to be fully centered in Jesus; from the unending repetition of exercises to the daily choices of obedience; and from the balance of discipline and freedom in ballet to the truth which sets Christians free to obey God.